1951-52
Western Nigeria Elections
-
"Carpet Crossing" Theory
Debunked !

Ayanti Udo Udoma

BME, BS (Math), MS (App Mech), MS (Telecom Mgt)

1951-52
Western Nigeria Elections
-
"Carpet Crossing" Theory
Debunked !

Ayanti Udo Udoma

BME, BS (Math), MS (App Mech), MS (Telecom Mgt)

Amazing Grace Publishers
USA • Nigeria • UK

IEI
Published by Amazing Grace Publishers, an Ikemesit Enterprise

Ikemesit Enterprises, Inc.,
P. O. Box 42, West Haven, CT 06516, USA
8 Dr. Udoma Street, Ikot Abasi, Akwa Ibom State, NIGERIA

ISBN 978-0-9819192-7-0
ISBN 978-1-7342415-0-1

Printed by Amazon-KDP
Designed by Ayanti Udo Udoma

While the author has made every effort to provide accurate telephone numbers and/or electronic mail addresses at the time of publication, neither the publisher nor the author assumes any responsibility for errors, or for changes that occur after publication. Further, the publisher does not have any control over and does not assume any responsibility for third-party Web sites or their content.

DEDICATION

He was a pioneer Nigerian Politician, a visionary of Nigerian Independence from Colonial Britain and champion of the first state movement (COR) in Nigeria

He was the Chief Justice of Uganda in the 1960s and the Chairman of the Constituent Assembly that enacted the only Legitimate Nigerian Constitution to date

He mentored me to always respect and uphold the unique ideals of **goodness**

To him, my father, the **Hon. Sir Udo Udoma, CFR** who inspired and whose literary legacy aids my writing effort, along with my great, great grandfather, **Ayanti Umo Idonho**, after whom the family compound is named and whose name I proudly bear, and **Abasi Akpan Enin**, the lead founding father of Ikot Abasi in Akwa Ibom state of Nigeria, the full name of which was Ikot Abasi Akpan Enin,
the following **Trilogy of Resolution Books** is dedicated:

1951-52 Western Nigeria Elections - "Carpet Crossing" Theory Debunked

The Go-Stop-Go Nigerian Republic - Volume II

O.J. Simpson Did Not Do It - Guess Who Did

P.S. : Proceeds from the sale of the Trilogy will benefit the **Sir Udo Udoma Library** & **Sir Udo Udoma Chapel** projects and their attendant education scheme.

Sir John Macpherson

Chief Obafemi Awolowo

Dr. Nnamdi Azikiwe

AG vs NCNC

TABLE OF CONTENTS

Table of Contents

Preface

"Ignorance and its denial will, sad to say, lead us down the same road as it did in all past history." ~ *Jordan Maxwell,* (An esoteric scholar)

The past and the future are other countries ...

The late Justice Chukwudifu Oputa gave us Nigerians, in sections **1.10 - 1.13** of his Chairman's Foreword, the following insight *vis-à-vis* the results of the HRVIC's probe, underscoring it with an observation by South African activist, the Most Reverend Desmond Tutu:

"We have to remember in order to forget, to learn lessons and to forge ahead. In other words, we must know our *terminus a quo* in order to arrive at our *terminus ad quem.* We must build on our bitter and sad past. This has been the *raison d'être* as well as the *leitmotif* of our work at the Commission. ... We, therefore, hope that the Report will offer a credible perspective on our past, while also serving as a road map for our future....

The following apt observation by the Most Revd. D. M. Tutu, Chairperson of the *Truth and Reconciliation Commission of South Africa* in the *Foreword* to his Commission's Report, at paragraphs 17-19 of Volume I of the Report, underscores this point so well that I quote it *in extenso*:

The past is another country. The way its stories are told and the way they are heard change as the years go by. The spotlight gyrates, exposing old lies and illuminating new truths. As a fuller picture emerges, a new piece of the jigsaw of our past settles into place. Inevitably, evidence and information about our past will continue to emerge, as indeed they must. The Report of this Commission will now take its place in the historical landscape of which future generations will try to make sense - searching for clues that lead, endlessly, to a truth that will, in the very nature of things, never be fully revealed.

The future, too, is another country. And we can do no more than lay at its feet the small wisdoms we have been able to garner out of our present experience."

Understanding "Carpet Crossing" in Westminster Parliament

Carpet or floor crossing is defined as an action in Westminster style parliaments, when a formal count is required, where a **Government or Opposition member** of parliament refuses to vote with **his or her own party** on the particular issue and crosses the carpet (the floor) of the parliamentary chamber to sit and vote with the opposing side. The term originated in the British House of Commons where the members of the Government's and the Opposition's parties sat on rows of benches facing each other and a carpet crosser having to cross the dividing carpet to sit on an opposite bench before the vote count.

An analysis of the results of a study of floor crossing in the federal parliament of Australia from 22/02/1950 to 11/04/2019 shows that:

295 individual floor crossers (2.6% of all MPs) crossed the floor for a total number of 1,519 times involving 520 issues. [**Floor crossings by independents and members of minor parties are not included.**]

Legislative and chamber procedural issues accounted for 25.8% of all floor crossings followed by taxation issues (9.6%) the environment (6.5%) and primary industry issues (5.2%).

No allegation of monetary or other inducement for the purpose of eliciting carpet crossing was noted.

From definition and practice, therefore, for any carpet crossing to happen, not only do the government and opposition parties have to have been predetermined, but so does the membership of each in parliament. There also has to be a vote count required matter in issue; the vote expressly **not** a conscience vote. Conscience votes, like to determine whether to allow euthanasia or same-sex marriage, are considered apolitical issue votes and hence do not require carpet crossing.

At the start of the maiden session of the Western House of Assembly on January 7, 1952, the government party was unknown despite the Action Group (AG) having won 38 of the 80 African seats. After election platforms were finally determined and party affiliations sorted out, the tally of seats was **NCNC 24 seats**, **AG 38 seats**, Ibadan Peoples Party **(IPP) 6 seats**, **Otu Edo (OE) 3 seats**, **Ondo Improvement League (OIL) 2 seats** and Independents **(IND) 7 seats**. (pp. 10-11) The first event that required a count of votes was the election of the leader of government business which event occurred later that day immediately after the **first instance of carpet crossing** of the house (pp. 17-19) leading to the election of Chief Obafemi Awolowo and his eventual appointment by Lt.-Governor Hugo F. Marshall as *Leader of Government Business* and *Deputy Chairman* of the Western Regional Executive Council.

Finally, **please**, **please**, it is *carpet crossing* and not *cross carpeting*!

Introduction

*"The way to right wrongs is to turn the
light of truth upon them.".*
~ Ida B. Wells, American inequality acticist

This booklet converts to a keepsake an article the author wrote
in 2014 for public consumption and critique but which five of Nigeria's
largest media houses (four newspapers and a TV house) would not
disseminate. It serves to correct a wrong that was propagated over sixty
three years prior by overzealous politicians who planted, in the Nigerian political psyche, false propaganda that had catastrophic consequences and that most did not have the courage to recant in their lifetime. Appendix F, included herein, is an uncopyrighted but related
and very revealing article culled from an interview given by an NCNC
politician of the period in review which throws light on the novice
practices of the first crop of Nigerian politicians, most devoid of constitution consciousness. Chief T. O. S. Benson, before he passed on,
graciously left us the piece to ponder and we are grateful to him.

The expose was titled "In the Light of Truth" as the author figured,
as Ida Wells intimates above, that the way to right the attendant wrong
was to turn the light of truth on it. Dr. Anthony Osa-Oboh suggested
that the title be changed, probably so as not to be mistaken for Abd-
Ru-Shin's *In the Light of Truth: The Grail Message.* The elections of
1951-52 were Nigeria's first experiment at democracy. The NCNC party,
led by Nnamdi Azikiwe, realising that the majority in the Western
Nigeria House of Assembly belonged to the Action Group (AG) party,
promoted, through his group of newspapers, the propaganda of AG
having bribed elected NCNC members into crossing carpet [no, not
"cross carpeting"!] on the floor of the House to AG to give it an unde-
served majority in the House and thus allowing it's leader become
the Leader of Government Business in the region, which black lie, despite Azikiwe's newspapers having paid heavy court fines for related
libel in the first decade, hoodwinked politically naïve Nigerians for
seven decades. The myth may, inadvertently, have led to the *coup d'etat*
of January 15, 1966 and thence to the internecine Biafra war!

To many people around the world, Dr. Nnamdi Azikiwe was an enigma, partly because, much as he is toted as being a successful Nigerian politician and industrialist worthy of the tag, "Zik of Africa", and who was the *de facto* leader of the progressive igbo inhabitants of the former Eastern Region of Nigeria by virtue of being the first premier of that region, there are none the less, quite damning red marks on his resume. For instance, he obtained the aforesaid leadership of the Eastern Regional government by means of what could be termed a civilian *coup d'etat*. His own "townspeople" of Onitsha detested him. For, instance, the administrator of the Eastern Region after the Biafra war, Ukpabi Asika, another Onitsha citizen, who allegedly had paid his University of Nsukka government owned and built housing rent "into Zik's pocket", called him disparaging names when he "crossed carpet" to the Nigerian fold from Biafra, where he had been the most consummate advisor of the leader of Biafra. This book not only debunks the carpet crossing posture of his newspaper group but, in its appendices, explodes for ever the myths of Nnamdi Azikiwe being the founder or a cofound-er of NCNC, being detribalised and, indeed, being a dedicated nation-alist. Appendix H depicts a brief picture of the prejudicial practices of this enigmatic personality in his hey days.

A brief introduction of the events that preceded the first ever nation wide elections in Nigeria and the first signs of the failures of the MacPherson Constitution which empowered Nigerians to vote for the first time is given in App. A, "Prelude to Nigerians' right to vote". Other appendices are an extract from *Who's Who in the Western House of Assembly - 1952* (App. B); a profile synopses of the Nigerian Ministers of 1952 (App. C); a brief attempt to clear up Azikiwe's murky relationship with the NCNC, whether as an activist organisation or as a political party (App. D); an excerpt of an address, captioned *Eastern Region, Nigeria (Commission of Inquiry)*, to the British House of Commons on July 24, 1956 by Allan Lennox-Boyd, Secretary of State to the Colonies (App. E); and the courts' take on the "carpet crossing" propaganda of 1952 (App. G) orchestrated by pro-NCNC newspapers.

The author has adopted the common signature of each of his authoring mentors, Sir Udo Udoma and Rudyard Kipling, of preceding each chapter with a meaningful piece of verse. This is the first of the *resolution Trilogy of Books* dedicated to three of the author's ancestors- **Abasi Akpan Enin**, the lead Founding father of Ikot Abasi in Akwa Ibom State of Nigeria, **Ayanti Umo Idonho**, the author's great, great grand father, after whom his ancestral compound is named and whose name he proudly bears, and his loving father, **Sir Udo Udoma**. Enjoy.

Preamble

Professor G. M. Trevelyan once said: *"Truth is the criterion of historical study; but its impelling motive is poetic. Its poetry consists in its being true. There we find the synthesis of the scientific and literary views of history.".*

From time to time, especially after a pre-Independence politician makes a public pronouncement with reference to an aspect of the Western Nigeria regional elections of 1951, the issue of "carpet crossing" comes to the fore and engenders heated debate. Sometimes, allegations of a "Yorùbá pàràpọ̀ (solidarity?)" creep in. But 63 years after the fact, no effort has been made by our now republican government to publish a true and accurate account of all the related events of the regional elections of 1951, especially those in the Western region of Nigeria. Such an account would have, hopefully, ended the debate and updated that chapter of this country's political history for posterity. It is not being inferred that it is government's responsibility to do so; just that it would have been nice and, indeed, productive if it did.

In furtherance of his commitment to the effort of trying to alleviate the perceived ignorance of the public, especially the youth, about the real constitutional provisions that have informed, and the machinations that have characterised Nigeria's political life, and to accept the challenge that a Senior Advocate of Nigeria has thrown at him, this writer will attempt, in a four part *exposé*, to point the searchlight on the truth about the proceedings of the Western regional elections of 1951, which were conducted under the provisions of the **Macpherson Constitution**. In the light of the truth revealed, we can, hopefully, allow ourselves to put the "carpet crossing" matter (and, indeed, its attendant "Yorùbá pàràpọ̀" theory) to rest, finally.

Serialising this exposé, the writer believes, will allow each section to be properly analysed, critiqued, rebutted and, hopefully, fully understood before the next section containing a major milestone in the elections process is featured. In that regard, the active cooperation and participation of the media outlets that will disseminate this exposé

I

is hereby solicited, with the writer's advance gratitude. This section, "Preamble", tries to highlight some important facts about the provisions of the Macpherson Constitution under which the Nigeria elections of 1951 were conducted as well as elaborate on the significance of one or two related events, which occurred on the eve of the elections and which readers should be mindful of as they peruse the rest of this exposé. Section B will deal with the elections to the Western House of Assembly. Section C-1 will cover the vote to elect the Leader of Government Business in the Western Region and, in section C-2, we shall examine the Western House elections to the House of Representatives at Lagos. Finally, in Section D, we shall strive to draw some meaningful conclusions from the entire exposé, with a complement of corroborating evidence. The polarisation attending the opposing sides of this issue can be attributed to several causes. But the most profound is ignorance of the provisions of the Macpherson Constitution itself. Sir Udo Udoma, (then E. Udo Udoma) as a Reid's Professor's Prizeman of the Law School of the University of Dublin, Dublin 2, Ireland, as an undergraduate student of Law, manifested sound knowledge and keen interest in the study of Constitutional Law and History, Criminal Law and the Law of Evidence, and it was his ambition to one day write a book on Constitutional Law.

Sir John Macpherson

After his postgraduate work, he became active in the affairs of the Labour party and the West African Students Union (WASU) while in England. As a member of the Labour Party of England, he lectured Labour Party supporter groups and joined with Mr. (later Dr.) Kwame Nkrumah, Mr. Jomo Kenyatta of Kenya, Dr. Banda of then Nyassaland and now Malawi, and Dr. Moody of London to arrange for the holding of *Pan African Congress*, which was to take place in Manchester in August 1945. He was elected vice-president of WASU and editor-in-chief of WASU Magazine and chairman of its editorial board. He attended all the constitutional conferences for the formulation of Nigeria's constitutions, presided over the Constitutional Court of

Uganda in the 1960s and, later, sessions of the Supreme Court of Nigeria, instituted as a Constitutional Court; and he chaired the 1977 Nigerian Constituent Assembly. He was an active participant in the political life of Nigeria during the period under review, an Independent candidate in Nigeria's elections of 1951 and was elected to both the Eastern Nigeria House of Assembly and the Federal House of Representatives. He studied and fully understood the provisions of the Macpherson Constitution and wrote about them in his dream book, "History & the Law of the Constitution of Nige-

Dr. E. Udo Udoma

ria", which is reference text in some university law programmes and which the writer will use, in conjunction with two other books by his Lordship, as the main reference material for this exposé. On page III of the unabridged edition of the constitution book[1], Sir Udo Udoma wrote of the Macpherson Constitution as follows:

> "*The most glaring defects in the constitution were to be found in the electoral system. In the Eastern Region, for instance, there was a three tier system of elections. As someone once put it, the whole system was riddled with electoral processes. There were three electoral colleges for anyone wishing to become a member of the House of Representatives at the Centre in Lagos. There were the primary Electoral College, the secondary Electoral College and the tertiary Electoral College. And these operated in this manner: members of the House of Assembly in the region were elected on administrative divisional basis of at least two members per division (secondary Electoral College), after they would have been successful in the primaries at the village or ward levels (primary Electoral College).*
>
> *For the House of Representatives, the Regional House of Assembly constituted itself into an Electoral College (tertiary Electoral College). Ministers, both for the Region and the Centre, had to be picked from the regional House in the former case, and among the successful candidates for the House of Representatives in the latter case. The primary and the secondary electoral colleges were representative bodies specially elected with the sole function and for the sole purpose of electing the members who were to serve in the*

regional House of Assembly. The elections (to these electoral colleges) were conducted on the basis of male adult suffrage in the Eastern Region.".

While the proliferation of electoral colleges in the Macpherson Constitution of Nigeria may have helped to confuse people, then and now, what is important to note is that there was no open vote to any office at the centre and anyone who was said to have won election in 1951 merely won a seat in one of the 3 regional houses of assembly, there to be one of 80 (somewhere between 90 and 135 in the North) members to constitute that region's electoral college for purposes of voting for that government's ministers and electing members to the Federal House of Representatives. The males who voted did so for personalities and not for party ideologies as they were unfamiliar with any of the parties, (except, perhaps, the NCNC which had existed as an activist organisation prior) which parties had only just been formed ahead of the 1951 elections for that purpose.

A common misconception about the regional governments of 1952 is the view that each was automatically formed by the majority party in the region or by its leader. That view is not quite correct. On pages 109-110 of Sir Udo Udoma's autobiography4 "The Eagle in its Flight" he writes as follows:

> "*In strict sense, no regional government was a party government having regard to the provisions of the constitution.*"

and on page 124 of his constitution book1, he says:

> "*Another important factor in this matter, to be stated with emphasis, is that, at the time under consideration, the government of Eastern Region, like any other regional government in the country, was formed by the Lieutenant-Governor, as stipulated under the constitution of 1951, and not by the NCNC party at all. The NCNC, like the Action Group party in the Western Region and the Northern People's Congress party in the Northern Region, was not recognised by the constitution nor by the standing orders of the House either of Assembly in the region or of Representatives at the centre. Ministers were each nominated and proposed by the Lieutenant-Governor and voted for by the House of Assembly, constituted as an electoral college. The government was formed by the Lieutenant-Governor.*"

Thus, saying that a particular party won the elections was a misnomer. It was a meaningless statement, especially if a clear majority was not achieved (i.e., 41 or more seats in the Western or Eastern House) at the conclusion of the elections since such a party was not recognised by the Macpherson Constitution or by the standing orders of the House of Assembly or of the House of Representatives. To expatiate on the powers of the Lieutenant-Governor, on page 257 of the book that he fashioned as the educated person's handbook for national integration, "The Story of the Ibibio Union[2]", Sir Udo Udoma wrote as follows:

> "*The Lieutenant-Governor was, under the constitution, designated President of the Eastern Regional House of Assembly, Head of the government and Chairman of the Eastern Regional Executive Council, constituted as an instrument of government policy in accordance with the provisions of the constitution. It was also the duty of the Lieutenant-Governor to convene and hold meetings of the Eastern Regional Executive Council to be formed after the conduct of elections in the Eastern Regional House of Assembly, constituted an electoral college. The members of the Eastern Regional Executive Council were known as Regional Ministers, having each been appointed thereto with the prior approval of members of the Eastern Regional House of Assembly by due process of law involving the employment of secret ballot.*
>
> *Among members of the regional Executive Council, precedence was accorded one of them as next in rank to the Lieutenant-Governor, as Head of Government, and was designated by the latter "Leader of Government Business" in the Eastern Regional House of Assembly. The Leader of Government Business was to promote and defend all government legislations, policies and measures in the legislature*.".

Another misconception arises in understanding the acronym NCNC. There was a transformation that attended the NCNC on the eve of the 1951 elections, and it is important to know the status of the NCNC before and that after the change.

On pages 113 and 114 of his already referenced book[1] on Nigeria's constitutions, Sir Udo Udoma wrote, respectively:

> "*It is not without significance that, throughout the period of the introduction of constitutions devised for Nigeria so far, no political party appeared to have participated therein or played any noticeable and effective role. Apart from the National Council of Nigeria and the Cameroons (NCNC) which, as the name implies, was in truth a national organisation and* **not a political party,** *as such, which protested over the introduction of Sir Arthur Richards' Constitution in 1945, nothing appears to have been heard of the existence of any political party nor, if any existed, of the role played by it even during the introduction of Sir John MacPherson's Constitution in 1951*.".
>
> "*The NCNC, no doubt, after the setback of the protest delegation to London* **had become virtually moribund.** *It was only resuscitated after the Ibadan Constitutional Conference by the incorporation into it, according to the publications in the West African Pilot news-*

paper, which later became its organ, of various national organisations, including some trade unions and ethnic associations in different parts of the country. Such various amorphous bodies throughout the country, as well as individuals, were specially invited and encouraged and, in some cases intimidated, to register by the payment of stipulated fees, with which to create the party fund, as members of the **new and reorganised NCNC**, *later renamed the National Convention of Nigerian Citizens. It was thus* **converted into a political party** *under the leadership of Dr. Azikiwe as National President, on the eve of the General Elections under the new Constitution of 1951."* Chief Dennis Osadebay later wrote in his autobiography[14] that:

Southern Cameroon, which had been ceded as part of the Eastern Region, seceded and reunited with the French Cameroun to constitute the Republic of Cameroun. The question of the name "National Council of Nigeria and the Cameroons" came up for review at the annual party convention held at Port Harcourt. ... I suggested that the party should be renamed "National Convention of Nigerian Citizens" in order to preserve the abbreviation N.C.N.C. which had grown very popular over the years and to show that we were **no longer a "National Council" of organisations but a political party**.

It should be, thus, incandescently clear from the foregoing that, to be considered a member of the NCNC party after its formation in 1951, (a). one had to register (apply or reapply) and (b). one had to pay the requisite fees. Conversely, if one did not apply for NCNC party membership or pay the required fees, that person was not deemed to be a member of the NCNC party. Even though the NCNC party was not renamed the National Convention of Nigerian Citizens until Southern Cameroon's secession, let us, for purposes of deferentiating the political party that was formed in 1951 from the then erstwhile activist organisation, use the new name in this exposé to refer to the party.

Further, anyone who did not satisfy the membership requirements and who registered and contested, instead, for another political party or contested as an independent candidate in the elections of 1951, cannot be deemed to have contested on the platform of the National Convention of Nigerian Citizens political party, even if he was the legal adviser to, supported by or a supporter and sympathiser, from time immemorial, of the NCNC activist organisation.

As intimated by Sir Udo Udoma in the last quotation above, the NCNC had become virtually in a state of statis in the years following the protest delegation to London. Expatiating on that, Prof. James Smoot Coleman wrote on pp. 308 & 295 of one of his books[3]" as follows:

"In the succeeding three-year period, from April 1948 to April 1951, the NCNC became relatively inactive and its more militant offshoots or affiliates failed to gain widespread support for positive actions. To some extent, the decline in overt and organised nationalistic activity was the result of new developments in British policy and of the situation that began to take shape in 1948 – the decision of Nnamdi Azikiwe and the other two elected NCNC members to abandon their boycott of the Legislative Council; the retirement of the unpopular Governor Richards and arrival of Sir John Macpherson."

".. and for the next three years the NCNC, as an organization, was virtually moribund. During that period its name and its objectives were kept alive only in the person and activities of Nnamdi Azikiwe and the pages of his newspapers. When the NCNC was reactivated in 1951, it was in response to a completely new situation."

Next, it might be instructive to note that, just like the NPC and the AG parties, the NCNC party in 1951, the year of its inception as a political party, was not nationalistic in nature at all. In fact, it concentrated its activities and election campaign in the Western Region of Nigeria, especially in the Lagos Territory. Its officers were the three candidates with the highest votes in the Lagos election to the Western House of Assembly. Sir Udo Udoma writes, on page 110 of his autobiography4:

"As the President of the National Council of Nigeria and the Cameroons (NCNC for short) in succession to the late Mr. Herbert Macaulay, Dr. Nnamdi Azikiwe converted the remnant of the NCNC to a political party *with himself as its leader and the party confined itself to Lagos and the Western region, Lagos then being part of Western region. The deputy leader of the NCNC party was Dr. Olorun-Nimbe and its general secretary was Prince Adedoyin.*

Udo Udoma, A. C. Nwapa and a third Parliamentarian

Indeed, most of the politicians who contested the election in the Eastern region contested as independents. For instance, Mr. Louis N. Mbanefo in Onitsha constituency, Mr. Enoch I. Oli of Oba also in Onitsha constituency, Mr. Reuben I. Uzomah of Orlu constituency, Mr. Alfred Chukwu Nwapa of Owerri constituency, Mr. Alvan Ikoku of Arochuku and Chief Ezerioha of Orlu constituency, who contested in partnership and cooperation with Mr. K. O. Mbadiwe to the detriment of Mr. Mbonu Ojike - all contested and won their elections as independents."

Further, says Sir Udo Udoma in that book, *"during the entire election of 1951, he (Dr. Nnamdi Azikiwe) had turned his back to the region (Eastern Region) and had never once campaigned there".*

Also, while the parties that were set up in 1951, as a consequence of the introduction of the Macpherson Constitution, may have been duly registered with government authorities, government had no way of knowing on what platforms the election candidates planned to contest the elections. In addition, candidates were allowed to contest election without affiliating with any political party, i.e., as Independents. Therefore, the Government Public Relations Officer, Mr. Henry Cooper, had to write requesting that each party presenting candidates for the Western House of Assembly elections should submit a list of its candidates to government, his request having been published on the front page of the *Daily Times* of Friday, 21 September 1951. While the interested public was able to read the names of successful candidates at the elections in the newspapers, it was impossible for anyone to conclusively determine the platforms on which the successful candidates contested (except the AG and IPP legislators) until those platforms were announced on the first day that the House of Assembly met, which was January 7, 1952. Thus, for instance, despite the fact that the *Daily Times* newspaper of November 1, 1951 published that Chief Adeola Odutola, who had contested as an Independent candidate, had in fact declared for the AG party after the elections, as reported by Chief Bode Thomas, government did not take heed of that until January 7, 1952 when the Chief, himself, first confirmed his election platform and then later declared for the AG party as we shall see.

Now, what does "carpet crossing" really mean? If it means the defection, in the House of Assembly, of a member or members of one or more parties to another for the purpose of their new party having a majority of seats in the House, or for the purpose of enjoying that party's majority status during the elections to the House of Representatives at Lagos, then it is in keeping with the spirit of the provisions of the electoral college system itself. Where there was no clear majority in the House of Assembly in 1951, members were allowed to align with another political party for the sole purpose of ensuring that that party had a majority of seats. Be reminded that, in those early days of Nigerian nationalism, there was no known political party ideology and people were simply voted for on the basis of their personalities. "Carpet crossing" in 1951 was not restricted to the Western Region alone. Sir Udo Udoma writes about the "carpet crossing" that occurred in the Eastern House on page 116 of his constitution book[1]:

"*Indeed, the majority of the candidates who were successful in the elections in the Eastern Region were* **not NCNC party supporters but independent candidates.** *Consequently, no effort was spared by NCNC supporters in persuading and prevailing upon the successful independent candidates to declare for, and* **join the NCNC party so as to enable the party to form the government in the Eastern Region,** *and also select the representatives of the Eastern Region for the House of Represent- atives, including members of the Council of Ministers in Lagos. Happily for the NCNC party, already, Prof. Eyo Ita of Calabar, a man of high rep- utation, had been hand-picked by Commander Pykenott, R.N. CMG, formerly Chief Commissioner, then promoted Lt.-Governor, to be the Leader of Government Business in the House of Assembly and Deputy Chairman of the regional Executive Council - an office later designated Premier of the Eastern Region. Partly because of the appointment of Prof. Eyo Ita to head the government and partly for the unity of the region, the campaign to win supporters for the NCNC party in the Eastern Region was successful. In that way, the NCNC was only able to form the government in the East under the leadership of Prof. Eyo Ita.".* .. and the carpet crossing to the NCNC of independent constituents.

While defection to another political party was allowed by the provisions of the Macpherson Constitution, resignation from a Legis- lative House was not. Once a man contested for a seat in either the House of Assembly in a region or the House of Representatives at Lagos and was elected, he was considered to be a member of that House until its last session. That is why the resignation from the House of Representatives that was tendered by Prince Adeleke Adedoyin over the issue of seniority in the NCNC party *vis-à-vis* the leadership of the NCNC legislators in the House, was not accepted. Despite being the General Secretary of the NCNC party, he had to serve under the Oppo- sition leadership of Professor Eyo Ita in that House.

Finally, on p. 118-119 of Sir Udo Udoma's constitution book[1], we find that "*... those members of the House of Assembly duly elected as members of the House of Representatives, as well as those members appointed Ministers in the Council of Ministers at the centre and known as central ministers, still retained their seats as members of the regional Houses of Assembly. There were thus,* **in all the regions,** members of both houses entitled to take full part in the deliberations and decisions of both houses and to vote therein. *They all served in the House of Representatives as a team from their respective regions. Needless to repeat that the position was the same in all three regions.*"

In the next section, we shall consider the actual elections to the Western House of Assembly and try to ascertain which party, indeed, won the majority of seats in the House after those elections.

Elections to the Western House of Assembly

"Democratic politics is a game of numbers involving the
counting of heads. There is, therefore, safety in numbers.".
~ Ibibio Book of Wisdom

The *Daily Times* edition of 20 September 1951, before the scheduled elections in the Western region, published that Nnamdi Azikiwe had boasted that the NCNC party would garner as many as 60 out of the 80 seats in the Western House of Assembly at Agodi Gardens in Ibadan. The elections, which were scheduled to take place on 24 September 1951, did take place in all constituencies except those in the Lagos Colony and the Benin area where riots necessitated their postponement. At the end of that day's elections, **72** out of the **80** seats in contention were won, as follows: National Convention of Nigerian Citizens Party (NCNC) **19** seats, Action Group Party (AG) **38** seats, Ibadan People's Party (IPP) **6** seats, Otu Edo Party (OE) **0** seat, Ondo Improvement League Party (OIL) **2** seats and Independents (IND) **7** seats.

On November 20, 1951, the elections in the Lagos area finally took place with NCNC winning all five seats in the Lagos Colony, thus bringing the tally for the NCNC to **24** seats.

On November 22-27, 1951, the 3 seats in the Benin area were finally determined with OE winning all the seats and bringing its tally to **3** seats. Thus, at the end of the Western Nigeria House of Assembly elections of 1951, the Action Group party won a majority with 38 seats while 24 seats were won by the NCNC party. To have **a victorious majority, at least 41 seats were required**. The 80 seats in the house, as announced on January 7, 1952, were broken up as follows: **NCNC 24 seats, AG 38 seats, IPP 6 seats, OE 3 seats, OIL 2 seats** and **IND 7 seats.** Here's the official list of successful candidates at the Elections (Source – "Who's Who in the Western House of Assembly, 1952²⁰"):

NCNC (24): Haruna P. Adebola, Prince Adeleke Adedoyin, J. G. Ako, Nnamdi Azikiwe, Theophilus O. S. Benson, Festus S. Edah,

Odeleye Fadahunsi, S. A. L. Job, S. Y. Kessington-Momoh, P. B. Nieketien, Yamu Numa, J. O. Odigie, J. A. Ogedegbe, Ibiyinka Olorun-Nimbe, D. K. Olumofin, G. B. Ometan, Francis Oputa-Otutu, Awodi Orisaremi, Dennis Osadebay, Obi Osagie, James A. Otobo, G. O. Oweh, Patrick K. Tabiowo and Fidelis H. Utomi.

AG (38): A. Adedamola, Isaac A. Adejare, Samuel A. Adeyefa, J. O. Adigun, Michael F. Agidee, A. T. Ahmed, J. Ade Ajayi, Oladipo Akeredolu-Ale, Abiodun Akerele, S. Ladoke Akintola, Cladius D. Akran, Tim A. Amao, S. O. Awokoya, Obafemi Awolowo, E. A. Babalola, S. A. Banjo, S. A. Daramola, Safi Lawal Edu, Anthony Enahoro, Sam B. Eyitayo, D. A. Fafunmi, G. M. Fisher, Sule O. Gbadamosi, A. Akin Illo, Al B. P. Martins, J. A. O. Odebiyi, J. F. Odunjo, Alfred O. Ogedengbe, J. A. Ogunmuyiwa, S. I. Ogunwale, S. O. Ola, Samuel O. Olagbaju, R. A. Olusa, J. O. Oroge, Arthur Prest, M. S. Sowole, C. A. Tewe, and Olabode Thomas.

IPP (6): Moyosore Aboderin, Adegoke Adelabu, Daniel Tayo Akinbiyi, Augustus Meredith A. Akinloye, Samuel A. Akinyemi and Samuel Owoola Lanlehin.

OIL (2): Festus O. Awosika and William J. Falaiye.

OE (3): Chike Ekwuyasi, Samuel Osarogie Ighodaro and Humphrey Omo-Osagie.

Independents (7): D. S. Adegbenro, S. A. Adeoba, S. Akinola, Sule Odukoya Hassan, Timothy Adeola Odutola, Wilfred Fentu Oki and J. O. Osuntokun.

The Government Public Relations Officer, Mr. Henry Cooper, who had earlier written to each party contesting the elections to the Western House of Assembly, requesting that it submits a list of its candidates for the elections (as earlier intimated), said at a post election news conference in Lagos:

"Of the winning candidates, the names of 38 were on the list sent to me by the Action Group. The six successful candidates at Ibadan were all among those who had been identified to me as representing the Ibadan People's Party. No claim of any kind had reached us about the party affiliation of the remaining successful candidates."

The list sent to Mr. Henry Cooper by the Action Group party contained the names of 68 Action Group party candidates for the elections, which list included all the 38 successful ones, and was published both in the *Daily Service* and the *Nigerian Tribune* on or before 24 September, 1951. Thus, it would seem that the other 3 parties, including the NCNC party, as well as the 7 independent candidates - D. S. Adegbenro, J. O. Osuntokun and S. O. Hassan, all secretaries of the AG party, Wilfred Fentu Oki, S. Akinola, S. A. Adeoba and Timothy Adeola Odutola that won seats, did not register their candidates or candidature, respectively, before the elections.

Sir Udo Udoma wrote on page 116 of his constitution book[1]:

*"As was to be expected, the real tussle took place in Lagos and the Western Region, between the NCNC party and the Action Group party. Although, at the conclusion of the elections, the impression abroad was that the NCNC party had won a majority of seats, but when eventually the House of Assembly met in the Western Region at Ibadan, to the surprise of everyone, **the majority in control of the House of Assembly were members of the Action Group party.**"*.

And, on page 351 of his book[3], "Nigeria: Background to Nationalism", Prof. James S. Coleman wrote that the victory of the Action Group over the NCNC by a sizeable margin, in the elections of 1951 in the Western Region, was the triumph of regional nationalism.

And what did the major victim of this purported "carpet crossing" conspiracy, Dr. Nnamdi Azikiwe himself, ever say about the alleged "carpet crossing" in the Western House of Assembly in 1952? Absolutely nothing publicly! Indeed, a cursory look through the 2001 reprint of "*My Odyssey – An Autobiography*[6]", by Nnamdi Azikiwe, reveals nothing at all about his political life as there is nothing on the "Contents" pages about it. In the "*Preface*" of the book, which section was written in London in 1970, he promised as follows:

"In a subsequent volume I hope to discuss how I founded the African Continental Bank; my entry into the orbit of Niger-ian politics; my participation in the crusade for the freedom of Nigeria; my stewardship as Premier of Eastern Nigeria; .... my tenure of office as Governor-General of the Federation of Nigeria, and then President of the Federal Republic of Nigeria; ...".

However, expressing his disappointment over the defeat, in the Western Nigeria elections of 1951, of the NCNC party of which he was the National President and first member returned to the House of Assembly for Lagos as a constituency, Dr. Nnamdi Azikiwe sneaked in on page 304 of that book - his autobiography[6] - under the subtitle **"The Zik's Group of Newspapers"** as follows:

"*The NCNC was under the impression that it had won the election with 43 members out of 80. As it turned out, 20 of the* **legislators who were known or regarded as NCNC members or supporters or sympathisers** *decided to align themselves with another party*".

He listed 16 legislators who "disappointed the hopes of the NCNC". It may be interesting to note the following glaring implications of what Zik was saying or not saying on pages 304 and 305 of his autobiography[6]. Firstly, clearly from what he wrote, whether or not the legislators he listed were indeed members, supporters or sympathisers, they did not all contest the elections on the NCNC party platform; otherwise, he would have referred to them as such or as successful NCNC candidates, instead of "legislators known or regarded as members, supporters or sympathisers". Now, which NCNC were these legislators known to be members, supporters or sympathisers of? Was it the activist organisation or the political party? Anyway, for Zik's declaration to be construed as meaning that these legislators switched allegiance after the elections, he would have had to say that he knew these legislators to have contested the elections on the platform of the NCNC party, which he did not. As President, he ought to have known those who contested on his party's platform and, hence, registered their names as requested, but he apparently was unsure, from all indications. Although he claimed that 20 people in his "camp" aligned with other parties (not necessarily AG), leaving a balance of 23 in the House, he only listed 16 people. Who are the mysterious four others?

But, let's just hold that thought for a minute here as we see the proof contained on pages 304 and 305 of Zik's autobiography[6] that Zik was not insinuating "carpet crossing" **on the floor of the House after the elections to the House of Assembly** as we keep hearing, but rather alignment with other parties at any time, whether **before the elections or not**. We will also see why none of the three numbers (43, 20, or 23) churned out by Zik is reliable if considering the former interpretation! Zik only mentions **16** people who he claimed aligned themselves with other parties and 16 is not 20.

Secondly, he lists 6 successful legislators as having joined the NCNC party after the elections – that is, as having declared for the NCNC party on January 7, 1952 on the floor of the Western House of Assembly. These people are legislators he did not count on at all – their seats just fell on his laps. They are J. A. Ogedegbe, G. B. Ometan, K. P. Tabiowo, G. O. Oweh, J. A. Otobo and Yamu Numa, who were among the 24 members that declared for the NCNC party on the first day. Thus, Zik should have mentioned **18** (24 – 6) and not **23** as the number of known NCNC party contestants who won at the elections since the 6 mentioned above were not "known NCNC party contestants". If we add 16 to 18, we have **34**, which not only is a far cry from **43**, but could not have been a victorious majority as he claimed!

Furthermore, since the 6 members above who declared for the NCNC party must have defected from another party or changed their Independent status to align with the NCNC party (i.e., "crossed carpet" to the NCNC) at the first session of the House, did the NCNC party induce them to so do? To be fair to Zik, yes, he did not comment in the book as to the 6 members being induced but, that is just like he did not say in his book that "the legislators who disappointed the hopes of the NCNC" were induced to defect from the NCNC party either, like his supporters are saying. However, none of those kindred soldiers mentioned that 6 legislators were "bought" by the NCNC in an effort to, "by that manipulation", try to allow Nnamdi Azikiwe to become the leader of government business!! (the words in quotes being some of the accusatory words used by one of those soldiers in describing alleged AG party inducement to NCNC legislators).

Zik also acknowledged that Adegoke Adelabu (who contested on the IPP platform) defected to the NCNC after the elections (just ahead of the vote for leader of government business), contrary to what one of his kindred soldiers is alleged to have said a few years ago before he died, as follows:

"*He (Akinloye) knew he was NCNC and* **his group (IPP) was NCNC. Adelabu remained NCNC.** *He stuck on to NCNC till he died.*".

So, Zik acknowledged the fact that Adegoke Adelabu did not join the NCNC party until after the elections; why or how is he then one of the 16 "who disappointed the hopes of the NCNC"? Hmmm!

One of the 16, a Mr. Coker who Zik claimed was a candidate supported by NCNC Iseyin branch, was not a member of the Western House, i.e., not a legislator at all! *Daily Times* of October 18, 1951 said that F. O. (Secret Document) Coker lost out to T. O. S. Benson in the primary electoral process and never contested in the elections to the Assembly. He subsequently left the arena to study Law.[8]

Now, out of the other 15 people Zik named, five - A. M. A. Akinloye, Moyosore Aboderin, D. T. Akinbiyi, S. O. Lanlehin and Adegoke Adelabu - contested the elections on the IPP platform (the IPP party having been formed at Mapo Hall in Ibadan in June 1951). They were confirmed by the Government PRO as duly registered before the elections as IPP candidates along with Samuel A. Akinyemi, just as Chiefs A. M. A. Akinloye and Moyosore Aboderin had both continually insisted in their lifetime. Akinloye also said that Kolawole Balogun, the then Assistant General Secretary of the NCNC party had delivered NCNC party membership forms meant for the six of them to fill out to become members of the NCNC party, but he had personally returned them to him unfilled, (confirmed in **ref. 19**) ostensibly giving notice to Nnamdi Azikiwe and the NCNC party bigwigs that they were IPP candidates. They added an exclamation mark to that notice by appearing in uniform for the first session of the House of Assembly on January 7, 1952. That leaves us with 10 people.

Two of the people listed, F. O. Awosika and W. J. Falaiye, contested on the OIL platform. S. Akinola contested the 1951 elections as an Independent but crossed to the NCNC party before the vote for leader of government business. Now, 5 of the 16 people published in Zik's autobiography[6] contested the elections on the AG platform and they were confirmed by the Government PRO as duly registered before the elections as such! Their names were published as AG candidates before the elections and there is no way that Zik or his party bigwigs did not know about their election platform! The 5 legislators are Arthur Prest, Anthony Enahoro, G. M. Fisher, R. A. Olusa and C. A. Tewe. Only 3 of them are Yorùbá! We are now left with 2 people.

Lastly, Chief S. Y. Kessington-Momoh and Mr. J. G. Ako contested the elections on the NCNC platform and remained in the NCNC camp for the election of leader of government business! As we shall see in section C-2, they declared for the NCNC party on Jan 7, 1952 and participated in the vote for leader of government business before aligning with the AG party just ahead of the elections to the House of Representatives on Jan 10, 1952, 3 days after the vote for leader of government business. Thus, we see that NONE OF THE PEOPLE LISTED BY ZIK WON ELECTION ON THE NCNC PLATFORM AND THEN MOVED TO ANOTHER PARTY BEFORE THE VOTE FOR "LEADER OF GOVERNMENT BUSINESS". Azikiwe hoodwinked the world!

Arthur Prest and Anthony Enahoro have been touted by "carpet crossing" proponents as the first NCNC party defectors to the AG party (perhaps, because they are the first two mentioned by Zik on his list?). But we read in Nowamagbe A. Omoigui's lecture "Benin and the Midwest Referendum of 1963"[9], with viable references, that, on April 28, 1951, delegates from Benin and Warri provinces attended the main Action Group conference at Owo at which the merger of the "Midwestern" and "Western" components of that party was accomplished.

Gaius Obaseki emerged as the Vice President for Benin Province, S. O. Ighodaro**FN** as Treasurer, Anthony Enahoro as Assistant Secretary, while Arthur Prest and W. E. Mowarin emerged as Vice Presidents from the Warri province. [*Oronsaye. Op. cit.*]. So we see that, as early as the day of the consolidation of the Action Group as a political party, **5 months before the September 24, 1951 elections in the Western Region**, these so-called "NCNC carpet crossing culprits", Arthur Prest and Anthony Enahoro, who are also believed to have, indeed, attended the inauguration of the Action Group party at the end of March 1951, were active participants and, indeed, officers of the Action Group party! And, it is difficult to believe that Nnamdi Azikiwe did not know this in all those five months or see their names listed in the papers as AG candidates. Also, they were not Yorùbá and hence could not have been part of a "Yorùbá pàràpọ̀"!!

It is interesting to note that, just as Nnamdi Azikiwe thought that 43 of the successful candidates in the elections in the Western Region were NCNC party candidates, the December 3, 1951 edition of *Daily Success* reported, under the caption "National Council releases names of Eastern Assemblymen", that the national headquarters of the NCNC claimed that, out of the 33 successful Eastern Region candidates on the list released as at the previous evening, 22 of them, including A. C. Nwapa, Alvan Ikoku and E. I. Oli, were NCNC candidates. That report is contrary to Sir Udo Udoma's assertion that most of the successful candidates, including Nwapa, Ikoku and Oli, in the elections in the East were independent candidates, and not NCNC candidates.

In December 1951, before the first meeting of the Western House of Assembly on January 7, 1952, Nnamdi Azikiwe, as President of the NCNC party, allegedly appealed to Obafemi Awolowo, as leader of the Action Group party (and the prospective leader of government business?) for a coalition government in the house. Anthony Enahoro, who was then the Managing Editor of *Nigerian Star*, one of Zik's group of newspapers, wrote in December 27, 1951's edition of *Daily Success*, under the caption "Zik's Appeal to Awolowo", as follows:

"*I have just read in the Daily Times what purports to be extracts from an open letter from the President of the NCNC, Nnamdi Azikiwe, to the leader of the Action Group, Obafemi Awolowo,* **appealing** *for a coalition in the new government of the West.*

FootNote (FN) - S. O. Ighodaro later contested election on the Otu Edo platform but crossed carpet to the AG party, as expected, on January 7, 1952 (p. 20)

It all seems quite naïve, and one cannot help being struck by the total absence of any really convincing argument in the letter for the coalition.

In the first place, the NCNC President now seems willing to admit that both his party and ours have 'a common foe and an identical objective' described by him as a democratic self-govern-ment".

Whether the "open letter" was fact or fiction, Anthony Enah-oro's write-up is certainly not the words of "a supporter and sympathi-ser of the NCNC" party "from time immemorial"! In 1960, Enahoro sued Zik's newspapers for libel and won. (Appendix G). Justice Fatayi-Williams ruled that ".. the defendant had **been reckless and had acted in total disregard for accuracy**". Secondly, by that letter Zik was con-ceeding election victory to Awo and the Action Group even before the first meeting of the House of Assembly, proving the later "Carpet Crossing" propaganda irrevocably that, and the resultant 62 year myth conclusively debunked by this author in 2014. Another response to the letter appeared in the January 5, 1952 edition of the *Daily Times* under the caption "A Reply to Zik – By Chief Arthur Prest", again before the election platforms were announced in the House on January 7:

Anthony Enahoro (Donning an AG Freedom for All badge)

Arthur Prest

*"… I then gave Mr. Azikiwe a challenge: whether or not he was prepared to retrace his steps, and if so, he was prepared to purge his organisation of the **fraudulent and deceptive practices**, in order that his political philosophy might bear good fruit.*

But Mr. Azikiwe has carefully and cleverly avoided any answer to this challenge.".

This reply by Arthur Prest, who is said to have been the sixth name in the membership book of the Lagos branch of the AG party at its inauguration on May 5, 1951, was certainly not from the legal adviser of the NCNC party of which Nnamdi Azikiwe was President!!

These two newspaper cuttings are "proof positive" that on pages 304-305 of "My Odyssey", Zik was not alluding to successful NCNC party candidates switching allegiance to the AG party on the floor of the house to allow Obafemi Awolowo of the AG party to become the leader of government business. He was simply lamenting - expressing his disappointment and/or surprise - at the fact that people like Enahoro and Prest, who had affiliated with him in various capacities for a long time, did not join the NCNC party after its formation and hence did not stand election on the NCNC platform, as he had hoped. Anyway, we now know that **no successful NCNC party contestant switched to the AG party between the elections and the first meeting of the house since the 38 announced AG legislators were all among the 68 AG contestants registered with government before the elections!!!**

In the next section, we shall delve into the events that occurred during the vote for Leader of Government Business on January 7, 1952. As earlier mentioned, movement of assemblymen from one party platform to another, for the purpose of forming a majority in the House or to facilitate selection for a seat in the House of Representatives, is one of the events dictated by the electoral college system that was adopted. To "cross carpet", in its real sense, one had to first be a member of the assembly and hence of the electoral college, and, therefore, the process of solicitation for same would not have started until after the platforms of the elected assemblymen were announced, which was on the first meeting day of the Western Regional House of Assembly (Jan 7, 1952). So, when did the "Ghana must go" bags change hands? During their lunch break? The foregoing points are important to note for, if mergers like Mabolaje (IPP)-NCNC, NCNC-OIL, Democratic party-NCNC or NCNC-Independents (which does not make any sense) existed before the elections, as Zik and pundits have inferred, such mergers along with the existing parties, were not recognised by the constitution nor by the standing orders of the House of Assembly in the region. If readers wish to familiarise themselves with the propagandist rhetoric, without due reference to the provisions of the MacPherson constitution, in Nigerian papers of the time, a good book of reference would be "The Price Of Liberty: Personality and Politics in Colonial Nigeria"9 by Kenneth W. J. Post and George D. Jenkins, which is advertised as the biographical profile of the political life of Adegoke Adelabu. No party merger group submitted a list of its candidates before the elections and whether or not candidates were pinched in their behinds and yanked away in speedy cars, to induce defection, is stuff for the movies!

PART C

C1 - Vote to Elect the Leader of Government Business

"Whenever the people are well-informed, they can be trusted with their own government.".
~ Thomas Jefferson

The 80 constituents listed on page 11 along with 7 ex-officio (colonial) members, including the Assembly President, W. M. Milliken, constituted the Western House of Assembly in 1952-53. The other 6 ex-officio members were Legal Secretary Noel Grant Hay, Financial Secretary A. G. R. Mooring, Civil Secretary Thomas Murray Shankland, Clerk Francis Desmond McGrath, and auxilliary members Robert Mc-Leod Barr (Nominated) and Hugh Spottiswoode.[21]

Characteristic of the parliamentary system, once the election platforms were determined, legislators belonging to the victorious party (AG) sat on one side of the House while the rest of the legislators sat on the opposite side. Here are the defections ("carpet crossings") that occurred on the floor of the Western House of Assembly on January 7-8, 1952 in an effort to allow a majority party to emerge.

Independents: Pursuant to the bye-laws of the AG party in 1951, employees of the party, including secretaries, could not be sponsored for the elections by the party. Consequently, D. S. Adegbenro, S. O. Hassan and J. O. Osuntokun contested the elections as Independents though their allegiance laid with the AG party. Thus, it was natural for them to immediately align with the AG party on January 7, 1952 and lift its tally to **41** – a victorious majority right away! A fourth Independent candidate, Timothy Adeola Odutola, also crossed to the AG party. At the end of proceedings, there were **3** Independent seats left in the House.

OE: Chike Ekwuyasi and Humphrey Omo-Osagie went to the NCNC party while Samuel Osarogie Ighodaro, who was already affiliated with the AG party as an office holder but contested election, by special arrangement, with Otu Edo, crossed to the AG party. At the end of proceedings, there were no OE party seats left in the House.

OIL: Festus O. Awosika joined the AG party. At the end of proceedings, W. J. Falaiye, the *West African Pilot* correspondent, held the only OIL party seat in the House.

IPP: Adegoke Adelabu joined the NCNC party while the other five IPP Assemblymen - Moyosore Aboderin, Daniel Tayo Akinbiyi, Augustus M. A. Akinloye, Samuel Akinwale Akinyemi, and Samuel Owoola Lanlehin chose to affiliate with the Action Group party. At the end of proceedings, there were no IPP seats left in the House.

AG: There were no AG party defections on January 7, 1952 while its secretaries, D. S. Adegbenro, J. O. Osuntokun and S. O. Hassan, as well as new converts T. A. Odutola, S. O. Ighodaro and F. O. Awosika raised the AG party's number of seats to **44**. At this juncture, because of continued bickering by the NCNC party members over alleged inducement having been offered to these converts to change their loyalty, Obafemi Awolowo procured the certifications to the contrary and the signatures of all 44 members on a declaration form and published them on photostat sheets. At the bottom of page 116 of Prof. Richard L. Sklar's book[8], "Nigerian Political Parties: Power in an Emergent African Nation", he says that the NCNC party described the signatures as forgeries. Later, A. M. A. Akinloye, D. T. Akinbiyi, S. O. Lanlehin, Moyosore Aboderin and S. A. Akinyemi, converts from the IPP party after an initial sit-tight, raised the AG party's number of seats to **49** (a clear majority), thus enabling its leader, Obafemi Awolowo, to become the Leader of Government Business in the Western Region of Nigeria in January 1952. All 49 donned on AG "Freedom for All" badges the next day.

NCNC: There were no NCNC party defections on January 7, 1952; new converts Humphrey Omo-Osagie, Chike Ekwuyasi, and Adegoke Adelabu raised the NCNC party's number of seats to **27**.

The configuration of Nigerians in the Western House of Assembly at the end of proceedings of its Jan 7-9, 1952 sessions, held for the sole purpose of determining a majority party in the House, was **AG 49 seats**, **NCNC 27 seats**, **OIL 1 seat** and **IND 3 seats**. The *Daily Times* newspaper of Jan 10, 1952 wrote:

> *"Once and for all, the "mystery" of the strength of the parties in the Western House of Assembly has been solved."*

The evening edition of the *Nigerian Star* of January 10, 1952, on the other hand, announced "49 GROUPERS IN WESTERN HOUSE" and followed up the caption with:

> *"Before the Western House of Assembly met here today, 49 members of the House with Action Group* (Freedom for All) *badges (e.g., p. 17) posed for a photograph outside the house".*

As we can see from the above, **no member who stood election on the NCNC platform in the West left the party to align with any other party**, not to talk of the AG party, to allow that party's leader to win the nomination for the office of Leader of Government Business and form the government of the Western Region of Nigeria. As intimated in section A, according to the stipulation in the Macpherson Constitution, the government of the region was formed by the Lieutenant-Governor.

On page 116 of his constitution book[1], Sir Udo Udoma wrote:

> *"The government of the Western Region had therefore to be formed by that party (AG) with Mr. (later Chief) Obafemi Awolowo, its leader, as Leader of Government Business in the Western Regional House of Assembly and Deputy Chairman of the regional Executive Council, an office equivalent to the office of Premier of Western Region".*

Please, note that, while the above may seem to give the impression that it was automatically the responsibility of the majority party to form the regional government or that the leader of the majority party automatically became the Leader of Government Business, neither was the case, as we saw in section A. Having a majority of seats in the House just made it easier for the Lieutenant-Governor to lean towards that party in his nominations and for the majority party laden electoral college to propagate that leaning in their voting. The Lieutenant-Governor also had the prerogative to invite the majority government to form the government of the Region. For instance, the Leader of Government Business in the Eastern Region, Prof. Eyo Ita, was not the leader of the NCNC, the majority party in that Regional House, as we well know and we have read that he was hand-picked by his Lieutenant-Governor, even before there was a majority party in the House. Also, on pages 138-139 of his book titled "Constitutional developments in Nigeria: An analytical study of Nigeria's Constitution-making developments and the historical and political factors that affected constitutional change[7]", Kalu Ezera says:

"In the Western Region, for instance, the nine African ministers were appointed by the Lieutenant-Governor (Sir Hugo F.
Marshall) from the ranks of the majority Action Group party in
the Western House of Assembly. Awolowo, the leader of the party,
became the Minister of Local Government (& Finance).".

So, we have seen that the majority party emerged during the
very first day in the life of the Western House of Assembly, that day
being Monday, January 7, 1952. **The AG party did not need even one
NCNC vote – the thirty-eight legislators who contested on its
platform and its three secretaries were all they required!**

In the next section, we will tackle the proceedings for electing
members to the Federal House of Representatives, which event, in
the Western House of Assembly, took place on January 10, 1952. There
were reports that claim that the NCNC party made several attempts to
pre-empt this vote by the electoral college, in the case of Lagos Colony
legislators, in the mistaken belief that since the five contestants for
the two positions were NCNC party members, the party could decide
which two occupied the seats. "*Cunny-cunny*"!EN Very Zik-like!! Suffice
it to include here two of those newspaper reports. In the Wednesday,
December 19, 1951 edition of the *Daily Success*, it was reported that:

"*The national headquarters of the NCNC announced that a
meeting of the central working committee of NCNC, co-opting
Demo Alliance councillors of Lagos Town Council, held on
December 14, 1951, decided that the two assemblymen to represent
Lagos in the central legislature are Dr. the Honourable Nnamdi
Azikiwe and Prince the Honourable Adeleke Adedoyin.*".

Later, the NNDC executives made their own resolution which
was reported in the *Daily Times* of January 4, 1952 under the caption
"Demo Executive decides in favour of Dr. Nimbe":

"*The Nigerian National Democratic Party at an Executive
Committee meeting held on Wednesday night at Pa Willough-
by's house, Lagos, decided that Dr. Azikiwe and Dr. Ibiyi-
nka Olorun-Nimbe should go to the House of Representatives.
Thus, the party reversed the previous decision of the NCNC
National Working Committee and of the NCNC, Lagos branch
that Dr. Azikiwe and Prince Adedoyin should go to the Central
House.*".

C2 - Nomination of Members to the Federal House of Representatives

Members of the Western Regional House of Assembly met on January 10, 1952 to elect members of the Federal House of Representatives at Lagos from amongst themselves.

On pages 116-117 of Sir Udo Udoma's constitution book[1], we find:

"*Furthermore, in the Western Regional House of Assembly constituted as an electoral college, Dr. Nnamdi Azikiwe, the leader of the NCNC party and first member returned for Lagos as a constituency, became one of the candidates seeking to represent Lagos in the House of Representatives in Lagos. Out of the five Lagos members returned to the Western Regional House of Assembly in Ibadan, only two were to be elected to go to the House of Representatives as members.*"

As a reminder, at the beginning of proceedings on that day, the configuration of the Western House of Assembly was **AG 49 seats**, **NCNC 27 seats**, **IND 3 seats** and **OIL 1 seat**. As earlier mentioned, the spirit of the provisions of the Macpherson Constitution allowed any assemblyman, not a member of the party in government but wishing to proceed to the House of Representatives, to align with ("cross carpet" to) that party on this day before the House of Representatives vote. As a member of the party in government, that member's chances of being selected by his new party, which would have the majority number of seats in the house, would be enhanced during the vote.

Three NCNC party members of the House of Assembly changed party allegiance on that day ahead of the House of Representatives vote. S. Y. Kessington-Momoh, J. G. Ako, and Awodi Orisaremi desired to run for the House of Representatives and needed Action Group party votes. So did S. Akinola and W. F. Oki who had both occupied Independent seats. W. J. Falaiye, who was holding the only Ondo Improvement League party seat in the house, perhaps to consolidate his employment as *West African Pilot* correspondent, decided to join the NCNC party. Those six were the "carpet-crossings" recorded on 10 January 1952 prior to the House of Representatives vote, making the seat tally in the house **NCNC 25, AG 54, IND 1**. S. A. Adeoba held the only IND seat in the House. There was no OIL seat left.

The election of members of the Western House of Assembly to the Federal House of Representatives at Lagos then took place. Notable amongst the results was that, out of the three former NCNC members who "crossed carpet" to the AG party before the vote, Chief S. Y. Kessington-Momoh and J. G. Ako were elected; Awodi Orisaremi was not.

Out of the two former Independents, S. Akinola was elected; W. F. Oki was not. Also, out of the five Lagos NCNC members of the House, Prince Adeleke Adedoyin (67 votes) and Dr. Olorun-Nimbe (51 votes) were elected to go to the House of Representatives as members, while Dr. Nnamdi Azikiwe (21 votes) was not, adding to the woes of the NCNC party. [Please, note that there were **two NCNC members**, Zik's own party members, aside from the victorious Adedoyin and Olorun-Nimbe, who did not vote for him, their party president.] This was in spite of the resolution of the party, firstly that Azikiwe and Adedoyin would be their representatives and, later, that Zik and Olorun-Nimbe would advance, and its contention that the electoral college vote for the Lagos Colony representatives would be unnecessary. But, receiving only 21 votes as against 67 for Adedoyin and 51 for Olorun-Nimbe, was not as a result of any outside interference; "**This was a punching bag that punched back**! The January 11, 1952 edition of the *Daily Times* carried the sub-headline: "DR. NIMBE & ADEDOYIN WILL REPRESENT LAGOS; ZIK KNOCKED OUT!". Sir Udo Udoma wrote in his constitution book[1] on page 117:

> "The defeat of the NCNC party leader in the Western House of Assembly found the NCNC party in the Western Region and Lagos in complete disarray. The party and its leadership were stunned. They were dumbfounded. Such a defeat was unexpected. More so was the defeat of Dr. Nnamdi Azikiwe in the Western House during the elections to the House of Representatives, since the contest was amongst five NCNC party members - Dr. Olorun-Nimbe, Prince Adedoyin, Mr. T. O. S. Benson, Mr. H. P. Adebola and himself, Dr. Nnamdi Azikiwe, the last of whom had had the highest votes at their Lagos constituency elections."

And on page 112 of his autobiography[4], he wrote:

> "Dr. Nnamdi Azikiwe's political activities as a parliamentarian had perforce to be restricted to the Western House of Assembly where he was least effective or harmful.".

The 31 members of the Western House of Assembly who also won seats in the Federal House of Representatives are: M. Aboderin, A. Adedamola, A. Adedoyin, D. S. Adegbenro, M. F. Agidee, O. Akeredolu-Ale, D. T. Akinbiyi, S. Akinola, S. L. Akintola, J. G. Ako, S. O. Awokoya, Obafemi Awolowo, F. O. Awosika, E. A. Babalola, Safi L. Edu, Anthony Enahoro, D. A. Fafunmi, Godonu M. Fisher, S. O. Gbadamosi, S. O. Ighodaro, S. Y. Kessington-Momoh, T. A. Odutola, A. O. Ogedengbe, S. O. Olagbaju, I. Olorunnimbe, F. Oputa-Otutu, J. O. Oroge, D. C. Osadebay, Arthur Prest, C. A. Tewe, and A. Bode Thomas.

After the Federal House of Representatives vote, Awodi Orisaremi, one of the three NCNC party members who had "crossed carpet" to the AG party earlier in the day but who failed to secure a seat in the House of Representatives at Lagos, went back to the NCNC party. The configuration of the Western House of Assembly at the end of proceedings of its session held on January 10, 1952 for the sole purpose of selecting members for the House of Representatives at Lagos was **AG 53 seats**, **NCNC 26 seats**, and **IND 1 seat**.

On page 117 of Richard L. Sklar's book[8], we find:

"*Mischievously, the Action Group majority voted Dr. Olorun-Nimbe and Prince Adedoyin, neither of whom would decline in favor of his leader, Dr. Azikiwe. In fact, Adedoyin could not be blamed because he had been chosen by the party executive to go to the Center with Azikiwe. On the other hand, Dr. Olorun-Nimbe had been given the post of Mayor of Lagos.*".

As confusion set in within the NCNC party following its President not being elected to the Centre, desperation followed. The party tried to induce one of the selected Lagos legislators into stepping down for their leader to take his seat. On page 117 of his constitution book[1], Sir Udo Udoma wrote:

"*For instance, a proposal to offer the post of the Clerk of the Lagos City Council, together with some other recompense and prerequisites, as an inducement to enable one of the successful NCNC party candidates at the Western Regional electoral college to the House of Representatives to resign his seat so as to enable the leader of the NCNC to automatically take the seat and become a member of the House of Representatives at Lagos, was blocked by a law of the Western Regional Government, which stipulated that appointment to such an office should be subject to the approval of the regional Executive Council.*"

The continuation of the piece above from page 117 of Richard L. Sklar's book[8], says:

"*In an attempt to bring their leader into the House of Representatives, the NCNC National Executive Committee asked Dr. Olorun-Nimbe to relinquish his post of Mayor to Adedoyin, also a Lagos Town Councillor, who might then agree to withdraw from the competition for the Central House and open the way for Azikiwe. Neither of the other two elected Lagos members, Adebola or Benson, would have stood in the way of the National President. When Olorun-Nimbe refused to relinquish his Mayoralty, the Democratic members of the Lagos NCNC and the National Vice-*

President of the NCNC, tried to buy off Adedoyin by offering him an appointment to the remunerative post of Lagos Town Clerk. Later, a commission of enquiry, appointed by the Western Regional Government, condemned 'without reserve' this attempted jobbery".

There was now no reason, Zik must have felt, for him to remain as the proverbial *lame duck* in the Western House of Assembly at Agodi Gardens in Ibadan. He thus tendered a letter of resignation from the Western House of Assembly and left the House. As earlier intimated, once a seat in any of the legislatures was occupied by a legislator, it remained occupied by the same person until the last session of that House whether or not he was physically there. With the "resignation" of Nnamdi Azikiwe from the Western House of Assembly, the NCNC party seemed to boil over in its aftermath. The party's Deputy-President, Ibiyinka Olorun-Nimbe, and Secretary General, Adeleke Adedoyin, drew so much flak from the other party bigwigs, for refusing to step down for their leader to advance to the Centre, that they both resigned from the party, thus reducing the NCNC party's number of seats in the House to **24** and increasing the number of Independents to **3**. The January 17, 1952 edition of the *Daily Times* reported that:

"*He* (Adedoyin) *gave three reasons: the attack on him in 'West African Pilot' of yesterday; the party's sudden clamour for three Nigerias instead of one; and what he called the 'party stabbing me in the back' last week*."

The NCNC party refused to accept Dr. Olorun-Nimbe's resignation and turned around and expelled him from the party, instead. Later, W. J. Falaiye, who had earlier joined the NCNC from the Ondo Improvement League party, apparently uncomfortable with "the fire on the NCNC party's mountain" and frustrated with sitting on the same side of the aisle with the feuding NCNC members, decided to join the AG party. The January 18, 1952 edition of the *Daily Times* published, in part, as follows, with the title line "**Another NCNC Member Joins AG**":

"*This means that the Action Group shall have 54 men in the 80-man legislative; NCNC 23 and three Independents - Olorun-Nimbe and Adeleke Adedoyin will join Mr. S. Adeoba as Independents. Dr. Nimbe has been expelled from the NCNC while Prince Adedoyin has resigned his membership in the NCNC*."

The *Daily Success* of January 21, 1952 displayed a picture of Zik, during the good old times at the Western House of Assembly, standing beside Prince Adedoyin and with Frank Oputa-Otutu, T. O. S. Benson and F. O. (Secret Document) Coker.

Here's some food for thought: Why did Zik not feature his political activities in *My Odyssey*[6], sneaking in "sour grapes" in *The Zik's Group of Newspapers* section? Why did he not ever make good his promise to release a "*politics and statesmanship*" edition biography? In *My Odyssey,* he admitted that his company, West African Pilot Ltd., was fined £10,500, plus costs in 1961 in Justice Olujide Somolu's court as damages for three consolidated cases of libels published in a series of catoons that alleged "carpet crossing" by NCNC legislators to the AG party in 1951-52, as a result of bribes given by the latter with plaintiff Chief F. R. A. Williams being its 'brain', plaintiff Chief Samuel Ladoke Akintola being its 'propagandist' and plaintiff Chief Obafemi Awolowo being its 'Fuehrer, respectively. **There was no appeal**. It is noteworthy that in his ruling, Justice Somolu pointed out that the defence of fair comment required that the material facts on which the comment was based should be *truly* stated and that the subject should be a matter of public interest. In his opinion, as the cartoons contained only allegations of facts without any comment on them, the defence of fair comment was not available to the defendants, as he said. In other words, there was no proof to the allegations, as we have herein demonstrated.

Obafemi Awolowo   S. L. Akintola

We will try, in the next section, to draw appropriate cogent conclusions from this entire exposé.

PART D

Conclusions Drawn from the Entire Exposé

*"Mockery is not always without its virtue; it incites
the person mocked to cultivate the knowledge of
himself".*
~ Ibibio Book of Wisdom

As intimated in previous sections, "carpet crossing", the defection of a member or members of one or more parties to another for the purpose of forming a majority government, was in keeping with the spirit of the provisions of the electoral college system itself. Where there was no clear majority in the House of Assembly, as in the attendant case, members were allowed to align with other political parties in an attempt to either get elected to the House of Representatives or to form a majority government. Party ideology was, virtually, nonexistent in the "wee hours" of Nigerian nationalism.

However, there were no NCNC party defections on January 7-10, 1952, during the proceedings for electing the Leader of Government Business, to any other party, least of all to the AG party. Thus, the so-called "carpet crossing" of Western Regional assemblymen who contested elections on the NCNC party platform to the AG party in order to allow its leader, Obafemi Awolowo, to become the Leader of Government Business, and his party to form the government of the region, **is a myth**. Ironically, the only House of Assembly where assemblymen crossed carpet to enable a party government was in the Eastern Region where an Eyo Ita led "NCNC government" emerged, despite there being scarcely any NCNC representation at the elections and even the "arch-exponent of NCNC party doctrines and manifesto", Mazi Mbonu Ojike, and his partner having lost to Independent candidates Mazi Ozumba Mbadiwe and Chief Ezerioha in their Arondizuogu constituency.

Also, in Sir Udo Udoma's words, "It should be pointed out that in each region the government was formed by the Lieutenant-Governor of the region. In strict sense, no regional government was a party government having regard to the provisions of the constitution."

Further, the writer has to agree with the pundit who recently wrote that the statement allegedly asserted by a popular pre-Independence politician that "Since membership of the House of Representatives was by an electoral college in the regional house, no NCNC men from the West came to that House at Lagos", **is blatantly false.** Indeed, it is a ridiculous statement for anyone to make since two officers of the NCNC party and co-legislators with Zik from the Lagos Colony, I. Olorun-Nimbe and A. Adedoyin, amongst others, made it to the Federal House (*Daily Times* of Jan 11, 1952). Two out of T. O. S. Benson's "five men of destiny" from the Lagos Colony, all NCNC members, had to go through to Lagos, no matter what. For edification purposes, out of 31 legislators from the West who went to the Federal House at Lagos, 6 of them were NCNC men, even though J. G. Ako and S. Y. Kessington-Momoh moved to the AG party from the NCNC party just ahead of the vote to ensure their selection. The other 4 are: Prince Adedoyin, I. Olorun-Nimbe, F. Oputa-Otutu and Dennis Osadebay.

Also, on the list of 16 people on page 304 of Nnamdi Azikiwe's autobiography[6], he includes S. Y. Kessington-Momoh and J. G. Ako as having "disappointed the hopes of the NCNC". As we have seen, they contested the 1951 elections on the NCNC platform, won seats in the Western House of Assembly but "crossed carpet" to the AG party, however only just ahead of the House of Representatives vote. They remain the only original NCNC members who "crossed carpet" to the AG party; but that was on Jan 10, 1952 – days after the election of Leader of Government business on January 7, 1952. W. J. Falaiye, also crossed over from the NCNC to the AG party but that was long after all House business had been transacted and all the "dust had cleared". He had contested the election as an OIL candidate. W. F. Oki and S. Akinola, who contested as Independents before switching to the NCNC party, also "crossed carpet" to the AG party on January 10, 1952.

From all of the foregoing, we can surmise that, on pages 303-305 of his autobiography[6], the "great Zik of Africa" was only lamenting that some of the people he affiliated with during the course of the activities of the NCNC activist organisation and the Zikist Movement, prior to 1951, as well as his professional employees, did not in fact join the NCNC party as he had hoped and, hence, expected. He was also acknowledging that while some legislators joined him after the elections, some also later left. By writing to AG to request for a coalition government, he demonstrated fore-knowledge of his party's election results. Zik was certainly not insinuating, in any way, that candidates contested the elections on the NCNC platform and then left to join ranks with the AG party to allow Awolowo to form the government of the Western Region of Nigeria in 1952, as pro-NCNC pundits and ex-politicians have alleged. His inclusion of S. Y. Kessington-Momoh, J. G. Ako, F. O. Coker and S. Akinola in his list of 16, even though three of them were in the NCNC camp for the vote for Leader of Government Business, while the fourth wasn't even a legislator, buttresses the point.

Dr. Nnamdi Azikiwe

Further, on page 157 of Kalu Ezera's referenced book7, we are told that, in his public speech entitled "The price of liberty", Azikiwe himself bitterly criticised the Macpherson Constitution which he felt was the cause of his defeat. He said nothing of "carpet crossing".

Mr. Harold Cooper, the Government PRO, absolved his department of responsibility for the "carpet crossing" controversy generated by the mostly pro NCNC party press after the election. Further, it is not true that Nnamdi Azikiwe resigned from the Western House over the controversy, as is alleged. In order to write to AG to request for a coalition government (pp 17 & 29), Zik already saw the "writing on the wall". By his own admission in his autobiography6, he remained, as *de facto* Leader of the Opposition, for the vote for the Leader of Government Business on Jan 7 and beyond. On page 305 of Zik's book, we find:

> *"With the remaining 23 members in the Western House of Assembly, out of a membership of 80-plus, the NCNC decided to go in opposition, since the Action Group had been invited by the Lieutenant-Governor to form the Government of the Western Region. The Government party refused to accord official recognition either to the Opposition or to me as Leader of the Opposition. Never the less, an opposition existed de facto and the Action Group could not ignore or extinguish it."*

Any talk of a Leader of Opposition or non-recognition by the governing party could only have arisen after the vote for the Leader of Government Business was held and resolved.

Further, Nnamdi Azikiwe continued to remain in the Western House in anticipation of becoming a member of the Federal House at Lagos despite articles like "The Ruins of an Egocentric Politician"

(*Nigerian Tribune*, 1/14/52). In fact, steps were taken, twice, in advance of January 10 to preempt the "electoral college" vote for the Lagos seats and ensure that Zik advanced to the Paliament unimpeded. Even after the vote had ousted Zik, the NCNC party tried two more ploys to get their party leader into the central legislature, where he would definitely have been appointed a minister and hence remained relevant. It is after these last failed tries that Zik became visibly distraught, necessitating malicious newspaper reports like "Zik – A Psychological Case?" (*Daily Success*, 1/18/52) and "Zik man (sick man)" (*Daily Success*, 1/23/52). No, the great Zik of Africa had too much resolve and pride to require a "shrink" but he must have found his drastic change of political fortune, within such a short time, unbearable, resulting in his having to leave the Western House where he would have been ineffective.

Thus, a statement like "Zik, the victor, lost" is a meaningless statement. As victor, Dr. Nnamdi Azikiwe topped the poll in the Lagos Territory and won a seat in the Western House; period! He never lost that seat nor would he ever have if he had not willingly departed from that House when he failed to make it to the Federal House of Representatives at Lagos. Nobody else took over his seat and the Opposition bench remained 23-seat strong after "the dust had cleared", as Zik himself attested to (p. 34), because Zik's seat remained counted. Zik did not record any other victory in the Western Region of Nigeria.

Similarly, a statement like "Dr. Azikiwe and his party won the majority of seats in the Western House of Assembly" is absolutely untrue, from all accounts. Mr. Harold Cooper, the government PRO confirmed the candidacy of the 38 AG legislators as well as the 6 IPP legislators. Thus, the election platforms of 44 out of the 80 members in the Western House of 1952 are not disputable. The remaining legislators had to belong to the NCNC, the OIL and the Otu Edo parties or were Independents. If all 36, including the 3 AG secretaries, declared for the NCNC, that party could still not have won a majority of seats since AG had 38! Indeed, the NCNC party could not have won a clear majority of seats in the West to facilitate Nnamdi Azikiwe becoming the leader of government business, **unless at least 17 legislators "crossed carpet" to the NCNC party from the other platforms, including the AG party**!! It would, therefore, appear to the writer that, if there were to be any controversy **at all** as to the above scenario, it should have arisen from suspicion of possible collusion by government rather than of possible inducement given by the AG party.

The writer has grappled, in his mind, with this next issue for a long time but cannot come up with an explanation as to why a seasoned politician, who is often said to be a Nigerian patriot and political pioneer, would make an inflammatory and erroneous statement like "Successful NCNC men who were not Yoruba were scared away (from the Western House)." considering that Festus Edah, Dennis Osadebey, F. Oputa-Otutu, S. Y. Kessington-Momoh, Fidelis H. Utomi, Obi Osagie, Yamu Numa, G. O. Oweh, G. Brass Ometan, J. A. Otobo, K. P. Tabiowo, J. G. Ako, J. A. Ogedegbe, J. O. Odigie, P. B. Nieketien and Awodi Orisaremi were all successful non-Yorùbá NCNC men who thrived in the Western House in 1952-53, two of whom, Dennis Osadebey and Frank Oputa-Otutu, advanced to the House of Representatives. None of them resigned from either legislature.

For 63 years, "carpet crossing" proponents have alleged inducement as being given to NCNC members of the Western House of Assembly to defect to the AG party to enable it to form the government and its leader, Obafemi Awolowo, to become the Leader of Government Business, the precursor to Premier, in the Western Region. We now read, from the records of an active participant in Nigeria's political life of the time, an impartial observer of the proceedings in the West at the time, and one who was thoroughly versed in the provisions of the Macpherson Constitution and who wrote about them, and from Prof. Richard L. Sklar's book[8], that, in fact, an inducement was offered within the ranks of the NCNC party itself to allow its leader, Nnamdi Azikiwe, membership of the Federal Legislature at Lagos, in spite of the rejection of Nnamdi Azikiwe by the electoral college on Jan 10, 1952. It failed to select him to fill one of the 2 seats allotted to Lagos in the Federal House. And, none of Zik's political soldiers has talked about **vote buying and manipulation by the NCNC!**

The bid failed because a law of the Western Regional Government stipulating pre-approval by the regional Executive Council blocked Zik's attempt to take over one of the two seats. As a result, he tendered his resignation from the Western House a short time after, without any consideration given to the promises he made and, hence, his abandoned duties owing to his constituents in Lagos. Following his exit, Adegoke Adelabu, an NCNC member, became Leader of Opposition which, curiously, would seem to contradict Zik's assertion that "The Government party refused to accord official recognition" to the opposition in the Western House. In 1954, with the AG party still in control, Dennis Osadebay, an Igbo NCNC member from Asaba, became Leader of Opposition. On p. 139 of Kalu Ezera's book[7], we find:

"Indeed, there were no instances of any bitter political feud between him (Dennis Osadebay) and the leader of government.

Awolowo referred to his opposition leadership as 'a sober, responsible and constructive one' and added: 'He and I have worked in perfect harmony without sacrificing a jot of the fundamental principle which divided us.'".

It would seem that Zik miscalculated by putting all "his eggs" in the Western House "basket" and ignoring the Eastern Region. Sir Udo Udoma wrote in his constitution book[1] at page 118:

"Thus, the situation in the Eastern Region was different from what obtained in both the Western and the Northern Regions. In the latter regions, the Leaders of Government Business in the regional Houses of Assembly were the original leaders and founders of the Action Group and of the Northern Peoples Congress, respectively. The government of the Eastern Region was formed by successful candidates who, on the whole, had contested the elections as independent candidates but were subsequently won over to the NCNC party by Professor Eyo Ita so as to be able to form the government in the region. As far as party hierarchy was concerned, therefore, there was a hiatus in the Eastern Region. The leader of the NCNC, as then constituted, who should normally have headed the government of the region, was left in the cold by his own miscalculations.".

[Miscalculations born out of his inordinate ambition!] No doubt, the political activities in the Western Region of Nigeria in 1951 and early 1952, following the introduction of the MacPherson Constitution, is truly "A Tale of Two Parties" in more ways than one. One of the parties appeared disorganised and unsure of what its campaign and organisational strategy should be, perhaps because it did not quite understand the provisions of the new constitution. It could also have been as a result of the three years (1948-51) of inactivity of the NCNC, as an activist organisation. Devoid of an election manifesto (unless "*cunny-cunny*"EN was it), the NCNC party resorted to bragging about its expected success at the polls. Its leader boasted before the elections that his party would win 60 of the 80 seats in the House and after the elections that it had 43 of the selected legislators, declaring in typical vein "we have won resounding victory in the Western provinces by firmly entrenching the NCNC as an undisputed majority party in the House of Assembly"[19] – all wishful thinking. We have seen that the NCNC party was unsure who was and who was not its party candidate; it did not submit a list of candidates as requested by the government public relations officer and it tried desperately to preempt the action of the electoral college in deciding which of the Lagos territory legislators would advance to the federal house, firstly by conflicting party resolutions made by different factions of the party before the vote and, later, by giving inducement to each of the two federal legislators selected during the vote, in turn, for him to step down for Zik. The NCNC almost disintegrated as a political party in the aftermath of Zik's inability to get into the federal legislature, the ensuing tumult resulting in the resignation of members of the party hierarchy and reduction of the membership of the Opposition in the Western House to 23 (effectively 22 since Zik had "resigned" from the House). Perhaps, that is where Zik got his figure of 23 NCNC legislators left in the House from in his autobiography[6], which would seem to confirm the writer's interpretation of what Zik of Africa was trying to tell the world in the two referenced pages of his autobiography[6]. Also, the NCNC party "flip-flopped" (*'cunny-cunny'*)[EN] on its campaign ticket. As Anthony Enahoro wrote of his professional boss but political foe in his article in *Daily Success* of December 27, 1951:

"*Whether the Lagos electorate really understood the issues inv-olved or not, there must be some of them who will find it surprising that the NCNC President, having won the election on a unitary government ticket, now advocates federation."* - "*cunny-cunny*[EN]"*!

Conversely, the other "lawyers infested" party, which Prof. Richard Sklar described in his book[8] as "the best organised, the best financed and the most efficiently run party in Nigeria" seemed to know exactly what it needed to do to succeed in achieving a majority in the house. Formed in March 1951, it published its mission statement on April 24 and had its official launching on April 28. It knew ahead of the elections exactly who its members were and submitted a list of its candidates to government ahead of the elections. Anthony Enahoro, in that aforementioned article said:

"*The Action Group had a set purpose in seeking a majority in the legislature. That purpose is enshrined in our policy papers."*.

Further, says James Smoot Coleman[3], on page 350:

"*The Action Group aimed at one specific objective: the capt-ure of power in the Western Region under the new constitution's electoral system. It differed from all previous Nigerian political organizations in several respects – (1). Its leadership was collegial, [Barristers Anonymous!] and this at Awolowo's insistence; (2). It developed a definite program in a series of policy papers dealing with all aspects of governmental activity (e.g., education, agricult-ure, health and local government) and pledged reforms if elected. (3). It developed a permanent organizational structure and utilized modern techniques of mass persuasion and electoral campaigning.*

(4). It shunned Lagos, partly because of Awolowo's belief that the city was a cesspool of intrigue, petty bickering and confusion.".

Finally, "carpet crossing" and "Yorùbá pàràpọ̀" proponents allude to "leading Obas and Chiefs", like the Ooni of Ife, Alake Ademola of Egbaland and Akarigbo William Adedoyin of Ijebu Remo, as being "drafted into the campaign train in 1951" and preaching "the gospel of tribe right up to the floor of the house of the Western House of Assembly on January 10, 1952" as if it were taboo for a chief or king to protect the stake that he holds in his society by participating in the political affairs of his people. Again, that allusion probably arose from stark ignorance for, while there was no House of Chiefs in the East, that being the choice of their NCNC leaders, there was one in each of the Northern and Western regions.

It should be fully understood that kings and chiefs have been active in the legislatures of Nigeria since the provisions of what later became the Sir Arthur Richards constitution came into force in 1945. Although that constitution only provided for a House of Chiefs in the Northern Region, four chiefs were appointed to the enlarged Legislative Council at Lagos from each of the Northern and Western regions. With the advent of the Macpherson Constitution in 1951, a House of Chiefs was also created in the Western Region and this time, chiefs were elected from these two Houses of Chiefs to the House of Representatives at Lagos.

**Alhaji Ahmadu Bello
Sardauna of Sokoto**

Sir Udo Udoma, on p. 114 of his constitution book[1] wrote that "in the Northern Region, the NPC was formed under the leadership

of the Sardauna of Sokoto (Alhaji Ahmadu Bello, believed by many
to have been, *de facto*, Nigeria's first Prime Minister) by a team comprising mostly of the leading men in the region". He also wrote on pp.
255, 259-260, respectively, of his Ibibio Union[2] book, as follows:

> "... *a conference of* **Mbong Ikpa-isong Ibibio** *(Council of
> Chiefs of Ibibioland), took place at Uyo which virtually drafted
> Dr. E. Udo Udoma as a candidate for the general elections in
> his constituency of Ibekwe-Opobo. In the circumstances, Dr.
> E. Udo Udoma had to bow to the popular wishes of the people.*"

> "... *a special Committee of* **Mbong Ikpa-isong Ibibio**
> *(Council of Chiefs of Ibibioland), ... addressed ... what ... was
> the most important Assembly ever held in the annals of the
> Ibibio State Union since its foundation in 1928. ... the Ibibio
> people were at the threshold of great, historic events and were
> approaching the goals which they had set themselves, one of
> which was to be able to select for themselves those who should
> be commissioned to act as their accredited spokesmen in Niger-
> ian Legislatures to replace spokesmen hitherto nominated for
> them by Government.*"

> "*It was necessary ... that their conduct, as worthy represent-
> atives and mature men of sound common sense, should reflect
> credit of the highest degree on the whole of Calabar Province
> as the ancient seat of learning, and, indeed, on the whole of
> Nigeria of which Calabar Province was only a part.*"

So we see that, during the period in review, participation by
kings and chiefs in the political affairs of the people they ruled or presided over, was not only in vogue, it was imperative! The initial entr-
ants to the political game were mostly inexperienced young men as
1951 was the first time in Nigeria's history that political parties were
being set up at the national level. The wise counsel and leadership
provided by the kings and chiefs, many of whom had been handed
down the experiences of treaty signings with, the giving of trading
privileges and approvals for establishment of consulates to and the
maintenance of good relations with our colonial masters, were inva-
luable. Perhaps, it is the participation of kings and chiefs in the affairs
of the Action Group party that imperceptibly determined the
divergent fortunes in "The Tale of Two Parties" in the Western Region
of Nigeria. The Ooni of Ilé-Ifé, Adesoji Aderemi, the Alake of
Abeokuta, Oladapo Ademola II and the Iyase of Benin, Gaius Obaseki,
were elected, as Western Region chiefs, to the House of Representatives at Lagos and Adesoji Aderemi was a Minister (Without
Portfolio) in the Council of Ministers.

Chief Adesoji Aderemi
The Ooni of Ilé-Ifé

It is worth repeating that **no successful NCNC candidate "crossed carpet" to the AG between the elections to the Western House of Assembly and the vote for leader of government business in that house in 1951/52; none!!!** It is also worth saying that continued hoodwink rhetoric like the paraphrased following by my respected Uncle TOS (Chief T. O. S. Benson), who has admitted to engineering the NCNC's "kata-kata" plan *[ostensibly, in retaliation for AG's vote buying and manipulation - NCNC's own propaganda?]*, the result of which plan led to the declaration of a state of emergency in the Western Region in 1962, one of the believed precursors of Nigeria's civil war, [see pp. 45-9] is not only most regrettable but is a continued exercise in futility. Further, the writer believes that Azikiwe not only realised this but so acknowledged in his autobiography (see page 38).

"*In 1952, the AG propagated its philosophy of East for the East, North for the North and West for the West, arguing that if an Hausa man was leader of government in the North, an Igbo man was leader of government in the East, then an Igbo man must not lead the government in the West. Of course, the AG philosophy gained ground.*"

"*All political parties played 'political games and rascality' in those days with the AG blazing the trail for others to follow.... In its 'political game and rascality' the AG, through* **vote buying and manipulation** *vaporised the NCNC majority in the House and this prevented Zik from being leader of government in the Western Region.*'

The real carrot in his veritable lesson underlays the following:

"***I was in the chair at the party conclave, which took the decision to confront and foil the Action Group in the House.***

.... *But unfortunately,* **due to over zealousness on the part of the executors of the action, things were not carried out as originally planned.**"

To borrow from that person of interest at the Foster-Sutton inquiry, we should be able to discern clearly that the voice in the above confession is Jacob's but the hand is Esau's.

This writer believes that Dr. Nnamdi Azikiwe did not have any intention of bringing out another autobiography volume, as promised in the *Introduction* chapter of "My Odyssey - An Autobiography" by Nnamdi Azikiwe and on its back cover. Also, he believes that Zik sneaked in the section about his disappointment at the way the proceedings of the Western House of Assembly turned out in its first week of meetings in January 1952 in an effort to bring an end to the "Carpet Crossing" controversy, without having to say anything publicly himself, both of the above being manifestations of his "*cunny-cunny*" disposition. The author has already demonstrated that Zik gave us enough on those pages not only to show that the so-called "carpet crossing" of Western Regional assemblymen who contested elections on the NCNC party platform to the AG party so as to allow its leader, Awolowo, to become Leader of Government Business, and his party to form the government of the region, **is a myth**, but to completely vindicate the likes of Adelabu and his Ibadan Peoples Party mates.

Further, in Chapter XI of that his autobiography under *Zik Newspapers and the Law*, he included summaries of the different law suits that involved his group of newspapers before the Nigerian civil war and his comments on each one. Two of those cases involve libel suits that were instituted by members of the Action Group party against his newspapers for "carpet crossing" related cartoons and reports published in them that defamed such plaintiffs. Nnamdi Azikiwe also reported the damages plus costs that were awarded to each of those plaintiff. (see Appendix G).

The words of two of Nigeria's celebrated jurists - those of later Chief Justice of Nigeria, Justice Atanda Fatayi-Williams in the case of *Enahoro vs. Southern Nigeria Defender* and those of Mr. Justice Olujide Somolu, the first Chief Justice of the Western State of Nigeria, in his December 22, 1961 ruling in the case of *F. R. A. Williams, Samuel Ladoke Akintola and Obafemi Awolowo vs. West African Pilot* should serve as further confirmation of the above myth. But more importantly, Zik's comments on same would seem to reflect an apathetic view of the incidents which would, in turn, seem to indicate some remorse on his part and a seeming intention to bring the propaganda to an end.

Justice Fatayi-Williams ruled, in essence, that the facts, as stated by the defendant, were grossly inaccurate, and so their plea of fair comment must fail, and that the defendants had been reckless and had acted in utter disregard for accuracy in reporting the results of the related parliamentary proceedings, and so their defence of qualified privilege also failed. He awarded £1,000 damages with costs.

Justice Olujide Somolu ruled that "... the publications complained of referred to the plaintiffs in a defamatory sense, and grave charges of fraud and other forms of dishonourable conduct had been levelled against them in those cartoons". He, accordingly, awarded £10,500, plus costs, against the owners of the newspaper, an award Nnamdi Azikiwe described as the highest award of damages ever made by any court in Nigeria, adding on page 352 "That it was awarded by a jurist who had considerable experience as a working journalist demonstrates the nature of these libels." Zik seemed to agree that "the political catoons" carried "innuendos of a highly libellous nature".

Going forward, can we, without sacrificing whatever dividing principles that may exist among us, live together in harmony? Could the ignorance of the facts, especially at a time of the lack of the globalisation features that exist today to make the world now smaller and hence better understood, have played a part in this "carpet crossing" controversy? Could the fears, suspicions and vulnerabilities of a colonised people of different nationalities, who were experiencing the political game nationally for the first time in 1951 under the watch of "prefects", have overridden God given common sense and hence allowed conspiracy theories to become happenstance in some people's minds? Is it possible that the "carpet crossing" debate has continued this long only because no accurate, logical, comprehensive and complete analysis of the provisions of the Macpherson Constitution, and how they impacted the 1951/52 elections, has been given to us in all these 63 years? Does Uncle TOS's near deathbed "confession" help any? Can we now see the events of 1951/52 in the Western Nigeria House of Assembly in their proper context and perspective? Are we now ready to put the "carpet crossing" matter to rest, finally and thankfully? Yes? If not, what has to happen for you to answer "yes" to the last question?

Seeing that some of us may actually have been complicit in propagating a 63-year old myth, what indelible lessons have such of us learnt from the experience? What do we really know about the everyday goings-on in the Nigerian polity? Do we really even care to know the truth about these goings-on? Thank you for reading.

Prelude to Nigerians' Right to Vote

*"The most important political office
is that of the private citizen.".*
~ Louis D. Brandeis

With the end of World War II approaching and as a climax to the changes already introduced, attention was turned to constitutional reforms relating to the governance of Nigeria. On 22 March 1945, therefore, proposals for a new constitution for Nigeria came before the Legislative Council in the form of a motion for debate. The motion was passed unanimously by the Legislative Council, its proposals being contained in Sessional Paper No. 4 of 1945. In par. 3 of the sessional paper, the aims and objects of the proposals were set out in these terms:

(1) to promote the unity of Nigeria and secure the **participation of Africans in the management of their own affairs**;

(2) to evolve a constitutional framework embracing the whole of Nigeria and establishing a Legislative Council in which all sections of Nigeria would be represented;

(3) to forge political links between the various semi-autonomous native authorities in each region with the Regional Council or House of Assembly for the respective region concerned in the former Northern, Western and Eastern Provinces, then called Regions, and therefore create direct links with the Legislative Council for Nigeria at the centre as the apex of this pyramid of legislative institutions;

(4) finally, there would be **African unofficial majority** both in the House of Assembly and in the Legislative Council.

For the attainment of the aims and objects herein before set forth, the constitutional Order-in-Council, 1946, which was issued on the acceptance of the proposals by the Legislative Council, defined Nigeria for the first time ever in terms of regions. The Protectorate of Nigeria was divided ultimately into the Northern Provinces or Region, the Western Provinces or Region and the Eastern Provinces or Region. As to be expected, the manner in which Nigeria was arbitrarily divided into regions without any reference to or consultation with the people was severely criticised. Regionalisation, being the reverse or antithesis of amalgamation effected by the British Government in 1914, therefore, caused considerable disquiet and bewilderment. There was public outcry - instead of unification, there was being introduced the obnoxious system of regionalisation with the tendency to reemphasise ethnicity or separate nationalities. The three regions thus created soon became bait for some aspiring Nigerian partisan politicians, in terms of leadership and as a means of gaining political power, accumulating

Sir Arthur Richards

of wealth or founding financial empires in tropical Africa by means of commercial banks - a most tempting material brandishment of colonial imperialism. The new enlarged Legislative Council, as constituted under what later became known as the Sir Arthur Richards' Constitution (so called because Sir Arthur was the Governor of Nigeria at the time and was known to have promoted it) comprised of 45 members, only 4 of whom were elected by adult suffrage.

The campaign against the enforcement of the constitution was spearheaded by NCNC, that's to say National Council of Nigeria and the Cameroons, under the leadership of National President Herbert Macaulay and Vice National President Nnamdi Azikiwe at that time. The NCNC successfully stormed the country, campaigning throughout Nigeria against the constitution and, under the leadership of Azikiwe, after the death of Macaulay in the course of the campaign.

Mr. Herbert Macaulay

Eventually, a delegation of distinguished Nigerians was sent to London and there protested to Mr. Creech Jones, M.P., then Secretary of State for the Colonies. But Mr. Creech Jones, true to British tradition in respect to colonial administration of supporting outwardly *the raj* on the spot, right or wrong, turned down the petition of the Nigerian delegation. He merely advised the Nigerian leaders to return to Nigeria to cooperate with the British administration in working the constitution. In spite of the rebuff which the delegation received at the Colonial Office in London and the coming into operation of Richards' Constitution, both in 1947, the agitation against it and regionalisation of Nigeria persisted unabated.

Mr. Creech Jones

Sir Arthur Richards, later Lord Milverton of Bristol and Lagos, having retired as the Governor of Nigeria in 1947, was succeeded by Sir John MacPherson in 1948. From 9 January until 29 January 1950, the General Conference, charged with the onerous responsibility of making recommendations to the Governor of Nigeria and the Secretary of State for the Colonies on the future system of government for Nigeria, met at Ibadan (headquarters of the Western Region). The conference made a careful study of all the recommendations made by the various regional conferences, as compiled by the drafting committee, and deliberated most exhaustively on the same. It then unanimously recommended, which recommendation was accepted by the Governor of Nigeria, and the Secretary of State for the Colonies, that a new constitution be granted to Nigeria based on three vital issues:

(1) Increased regional autonomy within a united Nigeria,

(2) Wider political, administrative and legislative powers to be devolved to the regions from the central government, and

(3) Nigerians, who were to form the majority in each legislative House, to be given full share in the responsibility of shaping government policies and in the direction of executive action.

With that aim in view, the General Conference therefore proposed that there should be a two-tier system of government for Nigeria:

(1) The central legislature, to be known as the House of Representatives, with a central executive council, to be known as the Council of Ministers, and

(2) The regional legislature, to be known as the Regional House of Assembly, and the regional executive council for each of the Northern, the Western and the Eastern Regions of Nigeria. There was to be established a House of Chiefs in the Western Region since there was in existence already a House of Chiefs in the Northern Region. No House of Chiefs was recommended for the Eastern Region and none was established or even demanded. The constitution, as finally approved, provided for representative legislatures, consisting of:

(1a) The central legislature for the whole of Nigeria, known as the House of Representatives; and

(1b) The central executive council, known as the Council of Ministers - members whereof were known as central ministers;

(2a) regional legislatures called the Houses of Assembly for each of the Northern, the Western, and the Eastern Region; and

(2b) regional executive councils of each region - members whereof were known as regional ministers.

Under the new constitution, Government, whether at the centre or in the region, was regarded as an instrument for the carrying into effect of the policy of Government already decided upon by the appropriate council. Government services had therefore to be reorganised in response to the needs of the new constitutional changes. Departmental powers had to be decentralised as part of the policy of increased regional autonomy. The civil service had to be insulated from political interference, the rights of the members of the service being fully preserved in that the Governor was made the head of the public service.

It should be recorded and acknowledged that, in the history of Anglo-Nigerian relationship, this was the first genuine attempt to venture into the field of federalism in the making of a Nigerian constitution; *that it was the Nigerians themselves who devised the new scheme*, and that the scheme involved the creation of quasi-autonomous regions and the devolution of powers from the central or general government in a unitary system to those artificially created regions.

In the scheme, however, efforts were made to follow the natural evolutionary processes dictated by the history of Nigeria, and efforts directing Nigeria towards federalism were even then tentative. *Had this evolutionary process of devolution of power from the centre to the regions been pursued normally and naturally by the further breaking up of the so-called autonomous regions into smaller units, it is highly improbable that Nigeria would have had the misfortune of going through a pointless civil war which was tantamount to an internecine warfare.* As would soon become manifest, this natural process of evolution was abandoned by leading Nigerian politicians who, as a result of the situation created by the constitution under re-view, saw the quasi-autonomous regions as British carrots too attractive to be resisted. Significantly, the lbadan General Conference failed to agree only on two issues. These were:

i) the position of Lagos vis-à-vis the Western Region; and

ii) the representation of each region in the House of Representatives.

By reason of these differences of opinion, there was a deadlock at the General Conference and, although the report of the conference was signed by all the members, there were four minority reports in respect of particular issues. Two of these were each signed by two members only, one by eleven members and one by twelve members.

Finally, the issue as to the position of Lagos in the scheme of things, as devised in the constitution and of the majority in the House of Representatives and, thereby, as to who should exercise control over the House of Representatives were, on reference, resolved by the Secretary of State for the Colonies in London. He eventually ruled that Lagos should form part of the Western Region and that the Northern Region should have the majority in the House of Representatives so as to exercise control over the House of Representatives.

One must wonder why no political party seemed to have played any significant role during the preparation of constitutions for the country except the NCNC which was at that time just an activist organisation, much like recent NADECO or PRONACO, and not a political party, as such. That was so because political parties did not become an anchor of the Nigerian polity until the MacPherson Constitution was framed. Political parties did finally emerge on the eve of the General Elections which were introduced by that new Nigerian Constitution of 1951, laying the foundation for the substance of this book.

It should be noted that a provision such as the one which placed regional representatives in the position of playing the part of being delegates of their respective regions in the House of Representatives, was a clear and distinctive breach of the fundamental norm of federalism. It is of the utmost importance that, in a federation, each government, whether regional or central or general, should be able to operate directly and independently of the other on the peoples constituting the federation within its own sphere of the exercise of power or function.[FN] This particular breach of the fundamental principle of federalism created problems for ministers and proved to be an obstacle militating against the smooth working of the constitution.

Ministers in the Council of Ministers in particular found themselves with split loyalty and under heavy pressure to call for amendments to be introduced even within the first year of the operation of the constitution. For instance, there was no provision in the constitution for the separate dissolution of any of the houses, whether regional or central. It was presumed that all the houses, both at the centre and at the regions, would run their normal course of five years. But within the first year of the operation of the constitution, the need for separate dissolution of the houses of legislature became manifest following Dr. Nnamdi Azikiwe's attempted civilian *coup d'état*, thus necessitating the House of Representatives to stipulate, after due debate, a provision granting Constitutional Powers to the Lieutenant-Governor, Eastern Region, to have the Eastern House of Assembly dissolved, in the event it should prove impossible to reasonably conduct proceedings therein in an orderly manner on resumption of the meeting of the house.

This introductory passage on the advent of nation wide politics and voting rights in Nigeria, as well as the problem that immediately beset the legislative houses, is culled from **Chs. 6 & 7 of "History and the Law of the Constitution of Nigeria"[1] by Sir Udo Udoma**.

There has never been any doubt in the author's mind that the greatest cause of the failure of the Nigerian nation is one of Nigerians' foibles, which is laziness to prepare adequately; i.e., in trying to run before learning to crawl, not to talk of walk. By failing to prepare, you are preparing to fail. One would have thought that once the first Nigerian legislators saw the flaws in the very first constitution they produced, they would have learnt from their folly and "righted the ship". Constitution consciousness is not imbibed overnight. If a Western House renegade goes to the Eastern House where he doesn't belong, how do you resolve the situation by empowering the Lt-Governor to dissolve the House and have fresh elections, instead of sending that renegade, who then turns around and installs himself Messiah, back to Ibadan? Why does the Queen's repesentative allow that renegade, a member of the Western House, to contest election a second time? Sirs Ahmadu Bello and Balewa were wise in demanding a gestation period before ushering in Independence, to prepare adequately before going into unchartered waters. The sun is not rushed by early risers!

FOOTNOTE (FN): When, in 2004, Olusegun Obasanjo unconstitutionally withheld payment of funds due the Lagos State government (for its pre-existing 20 LGs) into its Joint State Local Government Accounts fund from the Federated Account, the Supreme Court stressed, in a landmark judgment declaring illegal the federal government's action, that the federal and state governments are independent tiers of government and one does not superintend over the other.[15]

Who was Who in Western Nigeria House of Assembly[21] ~ 1952-53

"The happiest thing that can be said about democracy... is that it is one of the few systems that has been willing to risk a long period of confusion and mixed purposes for the sake of giving man a chance to grow up in mind and responsibility."
~ H.A. Overstreet

House Members (In alphabetical order)
ABODERIN, Moyosore; **Ibadan Division**
ADEBOLA, Haruna Popoola; **Lagos Colony**
ADEDAMOLA, A.; **Egba Division**
ADEDOYIN, Adeleke; **Lagos Colony**
ADEGBENRO, D. S.; **Egba Division**
ADEJARE, Isaac Abiola; **Oshun Division**
ADELABU, Adegoke; **Ibadan Division**
ADEOBA, S. A.; **Ekiti Division**
ADEYEFA, Samuel Adedoja; **Ife Division**
ADIGIE, J. O.; **Ibadan Division**
AGIDEE, Michael Frekede; **Western Ijaw Division**
AHMED, A. T.; **Egba Division**
AJAYI, S. Ade; **Ekiti Division**
AKEREDOLU-ALE, Oladipo; **Ikeja Division**
AKERELE, Abiodun; **Oyo Division**
AKINBIYI, Daniel Tayo; **Ibadan Division**
AKINLOYE, Augustus Meredith Adisa; **Ibadan Division**
AKINOLA, S.; **Ilesha Division**
AKINTOLA, Samuel Ladoke; **Oshun Division**

AKINYEMI, Samuel Akinwale; **Ibadan Division**

AKO, Jonathan Gordon; **Urhobo Division**

AKRAN, Claudius Dosa; **Badagry Division**

AMAO, Timothy Adigun; **Oyo Division**

AWOKOYA, Stephen Oluwole; **Ijebu-Ode Division**

AWOLOWO, Obafemi; **Ijebu-Remo Division**

AWOSIKA, Festus Olawoyin; **Ondo Division**

AZIKIWE, Nnamdi; **Lagos Colony**

BABALOLA, E. A.; **Ekiti Division**

BANJO, Samuel Ayodele; **Ijebu-Ode Division**

BARR, Robert McLeod; **Ex-Officio (Nominated)**

BENSON, Theophilus Owolabi Shobowale; **Lagos Col.**

DARAMOLA, S. A.; **Egba Division**

EDAH, Festus Sam; **Warri Division**

EDU, Safi Lawal; **Epe Division**

EKWUYASI, Chike Nwafor; **Benin Division**

ENAHORO, Anthony Eronsele Oseghale; **Ishan Division**

EYITAYO, Samuel B.; **Oyo Division**

FADAHUNSI, J. Odeleye; **Ilesha Division**

FAFUNMI, D, A.; **Egbado Division**

FALAIYE, William Jose; **Ondo Division**

FISHER, Godonu Midegbepo; **Badagry Division**

GBADAMOSI, Sule Oyesola; **Ikeja Division**

HASSAN, Sule Odukoya; **Epe Division**

HAY, Noel Grant; **Ex-Officio (Legal Secretary)**

IGHODARO, Samuel Osarogie; **Benin Division**

ILLO, A. Akin; **Egbado Division**

JOB, Samuel Adetomi Lucky; **Okitipupa Division**

LANLEHIN, Samuel Owoola; **Ibadan Division**

MARTINS, Albert Babalola Pedro; **Oyo Division**

McGRATH, Francis Desmond; **Ex-Officio (Clerk)**

MILLIKEN, W. M.; **President**

MOMOH, Kessington Salumany Yerima; **Kukuruku**

MOORING, A. G. R.; **Ex-Officio (Financial Secretary)**

NIEKETIEN, Peter Bieteiyeibo; **Western Ijaw Division**

NUMA, Frederick Yamu; **Urhobo Division**

ODEBIYI, J. A. O.; **Egbado Division**

ODIGIE, Joseph Okokhue Ahimejese; **Ishan Division**

ODUNJO, J. F.; **Egba Division**

ODUTOLA, Timothy Adeola; **Ijebu-Remo Division**

OGEDEGBE, John Ailoje; **Kukuruku Division**

OGEDENGBE, Alfred Obatuyi; **Owo Division**

OGUNMUYIWA, J. A.; **Oshun Division**

OGUNWALE, S. I.; **Oshun Division**

OKI, Wilfred Fentu; **Aboh Division**

OLA, S. O.; **Oshun Division**

OLAGBAJU, Samuel Olafare; **Ife Division**

OLORUN-NIMBE, Abu Bakry Ibiyinka; **Lagos Colony**

OLUMOFIN, Daniel Kubaje; **Owo Division**

"Who's Who in the Western House of Assembly"
Two pages of members' profiles, including those of the
protagonists, Nnamdi Azikiwe and Obafemi Awolowo.

OLUSA, Richard Aderinuye; **Owo Division**

OMETAN, George Brass; **Urhobo Division**

OMO-OSAGIE, Humphrey; **Benin Division**

OPUTA-OTUTU, Francis; **Aboh Division**

ORISAREMI, Awodi; **Kukuruku Division**

OROGE, J. A.; **Oshun Division**

OSADEBAY, Dennis Chukwude; **Asaba Division**

OSAGIE, Obi; **Asaba Division**

OSUNTOKUN, J. O.; **Ekiti Division**

OTOBO, James Ekpe; **Urhobo Division**

OWEH, G. Ohwotemu; **Urhobo Division**

PREST, Arthur Edward; **Warri Division**

SHANKLAND, Thomas Murray; **Ex-O (Civil Secretary)**

SOWOLE, Michael Soyebo; **Ijebu-Remo Division**

SPOTTISWOODE, Hugh; **Ex-Officio member**

TABIOWO, Patrick Koarurhiebie; **Urhobo Division**

TEWE, Cornelius Akinbowale; **Okitipupa Division**

THOMAS, A. Olabode; **Oyo Division**

UTOMI, Fidelius Harold; **Asaba Division**

Central Ministers

ADEREMI, Adesoji; **(Ooni of Ife); Without Portfolio**

AKINTOLA, Samuel Ladoke; **Labour**

PREST, Arthur Edward; **Communications**

THOMAS, A. Olabode; **Transport**

Regional Ministers

AKINLOYE, Augustus M. Adisa; **Natural Resources**

AKISANYA, S.; **(Odemo of Ishara); Without Portfolio**

AKRAN, Claudius Dosa; **Local Development**

AWOKOYA, Stephen Oluwole; **Education**

AWOLOWO, Obafemi; **Local Government & Finance**

BABALOLA, E. A.; **Works**

IGHODARO, Samuel Osarogie; **Public Health**

ODUNJO, J. F.; **Land & Survey**

OLAGBEGI II; (Olowo of Owo); Without Portfolio

Nigeria's Council of Ministers, 1952

"For forms of government, let fools contest;
whatever is best administered is best.".
~ Alexander Pope

Sir John Stuart Macpherson
Post: **Governor General**
Portfolio: **Chairman**

Sir John Macpherson came in 1947 as the new Governor-General of Nigeria. On assumption of office, he was full of praises for Sir Arthur Richards' Constitution of 1945, then in operation, to the disappointment of politically minded Nigerians. But, in 1950, to the delight of the generality of Nigerians, Sir Macpherson initiated action leading to a review of Sir Arthur Richards' Constitution.

He set up a constitutional conference, the majority of members whereof were Nigerians. The result was the Macpherson Constitution which was to allow Nigerians to, supposedly, govern themselves for the first time. Unfortunately, the constitution was incapable of resisting political pressure exerted by the politicians and ultimately collapsed like a pack of cards by mid 1953. It was then left to the Hon. Mr. Oliver Lyttleton, Secretary of State for the Colonies, to step into the breach and call up a new constitutional conference.

Alhaji Abubakar Tafawa Balewa

Party: **NPC**

Portfolio: **Works**

He was the deputy leader and co-founder of the NPC party and the Leader of Government Business in the Federal House. Elected Chief Minister in 1957, he became the only Prime Minister of Independent Nigeria in 1960, doubling as Foreign Affairs advocate for a year.

As Prime Minister, on his party leader's advice, he extended invitations to the Action Group (AG) and Northern Elements Progressive Union (NEPU) parties through their leaders, Chief Obafemi Awolowo and Mallam Aminu Kano, respectively, to join the NPC and NCNC parties in forming an all-representative government for Nigeria, and they each declined, perhaps because of their political differences with Nnamdi Azikiwe and Sir Ahmadu Bello, respectively. What a pity!

In his second term as Prime Minister, he was captured by the perpetrators of the *coup d'état* of 1966 and murdered.

Alhaji Adesoji Aderemi, KBE, CMG

Party: **Western House of Chiefs**

Portfolio: **Without portfolio**

The Ooni of Ilé-Ifé was a very well respected statesman who rose politically to become the Governor of the Western region of Nigeria. As Governor, he tried to dismiss the then Premier of the Western Region, Chief S. L Akintola, who had fallen foul of the leadership of his party, the Action Group. The intractable and irresolvable situation ensued from a dispute between the Premier and the leader of the party, Chief Obafemi Awolowo. The resultant court case, ref. IALL NLR Part 3 442-461 went all the way to the Privy Council before it was resolved.

Mr. Alfred Chukwudifu Nwapa

Party: **NCNC**

Portfolio: **Commerce & Industries**

There was a regimented campaign of a scurrilous kind against the incumbent NCNC ministers in the Council of Ministers, especially Mr. Alfred Chukwu Nwapa, who was also a minister in the Eastern regional Executive Council. Mr. Alfred Chuku Nwapa had to be singled out for sustained scurrilous attacks because he had become famous and was suspected, in certain circles in the old NCNC party, as deliberately being groomed, with the aid of British expatriate officials, to replace Dr. Nnamdi Azikiwe, not only as the leader of the NCNC but also of the Igbo people politically, since Dr. Nnamdi Azikiwe had been destroyed nationally and politically at Ibadan, by the AG party. The ground for the ill-founded suspicion against him was the regular publicity usually given him and his activities by the press, especially the *Daily Times* newspaper in Lagos to which he was entitled as the trade and commerce central minister.

Alhaji Mohammadu Ribadu

Party: **NPC**

Portfolio: **Natural Resources**

The son of a district head from Adamawa's Balala district, he was one of the team members comprising mostly of the leading and most powerful men in the Northern region who formed the Northern Peoples Congress (NPC) party, under the leadership of the Sardauna of Sokoto. A learned, powerful and intrepid politician, he was soon elected the second Vice-President of the NPC and later, while serving as Federal Minister of Defence, Ribadu saw about the rapid expansion of the Nigerian Army and Navy as well as the creation of the Nigerian Air Force.

Chief S. Ladoke Akintola
Party: **AG**
Portfolio: **Labour**

A member of the formidable team that organised the Action Group party, he and his colleagues in the council resigned from the House of Representatives following the events that occurred in Lagos on March 31, 1953, and the ensuing "walk out" and "historic embrace" by Zik and Awolowo. He was in the AG delegation to the 1953 London Conference.

He later became the Premier of the Western Region but fell foul of the leadership of his party following a dispute he had with its leader, Chief Obafemi Awolowo. Following a petition from his party, the Governor of the region, Alhaji Adesoji Aderemi, tried to dismiss him from the Premiership of the Western Region and he quickly took court action to mitigate it. The court case, ref. 1ALL NLR Part 3 442-461, went all the way to the Privy Council before resolution.

He was murdered by the perpetrators of the *coup d'état* of 1966.

Prof. Eni Njoku
Party: **NCNC**
Portfolio: **Mines & Power**

Member from the Umuahia-Bende divisional constituency, he was one of the targets of Zik's wing of the NCNC during Zik's civilian *coup d'état*. Later, he was a leading and foundation member of the National Independence Party (NIP) and it was he who suggested the name. He later led the delegation representing the Eastern Region to, and gave a presentation at, the Ad Hoc Constitutional Conference of Sept. 12 - Oct. 3, 1966 at Lagos, which conference had been convened by Lt. Col. Yakubu Gowon and Dr. Nnamdi Azikiwe, the latter being conspicuously absent at the conference.

Alhaji Shettima Kashim
Party: **NPC**
Portfolio: **Social Services**

A founding member of the NPC party, Shettima Kashim, later Sir Kashim Ibrahim, was a Kanuri politician who was head of the Native Administration in Borno, holding the traditional title of Waziri of the Emirate of Borno after two previous Waziris had been forced to resign as a result of scandals in the Borno local administration. A close associate of the Sadauna, he became the Governor of the Northern region in 1962, holding office until the military coup of 16 January 1966.

Chief Bode Thomas
Party: **AG**
Portfolio: **Works**

He was a member of the formidable team that organised the Action Group party in the Western region. He, along with the other AG ministers, resigned their seats in the House of Representatives following the abrupt adjournment of the House by reason of the episode which had occurred in Lagos on March 31, 1953, and the ensuing "walk out" and "historic embrace" by Zik and Awolowo. He, also, was a member of the Action Group delegation to the 1953 London Conference.

Dr. Okoi Arikpo
Party: **NCNC**
Portfolio: **Lands, Surveys & Local Development**

Representing Obubra Divisional constituency, he was a central minister and a member of the Executive Council of the Eastern region. He was expelled with ignominy and for life by Zik's wing of the NCNC party during Zik's bid to regain prominence in Nigerian politics.

After Zik's civilian *coup d'état*, he resigned from the NCNC along with his colleagues to form the National Independence party (NIP) as a leading and foundation member. He was appointed Assistant General-Secretary of the Calabar-Ogoja-Rivers (COR) state movement while the NIP party agreed to merge with Alvan Ikoku's party, the United National party (UNP) to form the United National Independence party (UNIP), and to have UNIP become an organ of the movement. He was appointed to several subsequent Nigerian cabinets. Like Eni Njoku, he submitted a proposal to the Ad Hoc Constitutional Conference of Sept.- Oct. 1966.

Alhaji Usman Nagogo, KBE, CMG
Party: **NPC**
Portfolio: **Without Portfolio**

Usman Nagogo dan Muhammadu Dikko, father of Lt. Colonel Hassan Katsina, was District Head of Katsina Metropolis Police when officially installed as the tenth Emir of Katsina by Sir Arthur Richards, Governor of Northern Nigeria, on May 19, 1944. He succeeded his father, Muhammadu Dikko, and was succeeded by his son, Muhammadu Kabir Usman. He was one of the pioneering personalities of indigenous Nigerian polo and life President of the Nigerian Polo Association.

Chief Arthur Edward Prest
Party: **AG**
Portfolio: **Communications**

An Itsekiri politician of mixed heritage from the Warri division of southern Nigeria, he was one of the founding members of the AG party and was appointed Vice President of the Warri Province branch of the party. Having previously served as legal adviser to the activist organisation, NCNC, he was very critical of Nnamdi Azikiwe on the eve of the opening of the Western House of Assembly, accusing Zik of fraudulent and deceptive practices. He, also, resigned his seat in the House of Representatives in April, 1953, following the abrupt adjournment of the House.

Dr. Emmanuel M. I. Endeley
Party: **NCNC**
Portfolio: **Without Portfolio**

He was the leader of the Cameroon team in the old NCNC, representing Southern Cameroon. Following the failed "motion of no confidence in the ministers" and prelude to Zik's civilian *coup d'état* in the Eastern House of Assembly, he along with the other NCNC Central Ministers, were expelled with ignominy and for life by Zik's wing of the NCNC party, because they were also members of the Executive Council of the Eastern region.

Later, under his leadership, the Kamerun National Congress (KNC) was formed under the Mandate of the UN Trusteeship Council.

Other Members of the Council of Ministers

Just as in the regional houses of assembly, other than the Governor of Nigeria, who was Chairman, and the twelve Nigerian indigenes already profiled, membership of the Council of Ministers also included twelve expatriate officials of status not below that of a Permanent Secretary, seven of whom appear in the photograph on page 40.

Misconceptions about the founding of the NCNC

"It is seldom realised that history cannot be cheated nor can injustice be obliterated with the wink; truth crushed will rise again in due time."
~ Sir Udo Udoma

PREAMBLE

The Internet and other sources of historical records are replete with inconsistent speculations (most wrong) as to the origin and founders of the NCNC, whether as an activist organisation, as existed prior to the adoption of the MacPherson Constitution in 1951, or as a political party, as was formed as a consequence of that constitution.

Wikepidea says: "The National Council of Nigeria and the Cameroons was formed in 1944 by Herbert Macaulay. Herbert Macaulay was its first president, while Azikiwe was its first secretary. ... The party is considered to be the third prominent political party formed in Nigeria after a Lagos-based party, the Nigerian National Democratic Party, and the **Nigerian Youth Movement, formed by Professor Eyo Ita** who became the Deputy National President of NCNC before he left the party to form *his own political party called the National Independence Party. ...* The **NCNC won majority votes in the Eastern Region** of Nigeria's House of Assembly [in 1951] ... the **party could have secured a majority in the Western House** of Assembly *if it had been able to persuade the third party*, which was an Ibadan community party and which had been viewed by the NCNC as its ally, *to support it.*" *Wikepidea* further describes Eyo Ita as the "**first Nigerian professor**".

Now, the **NCNC was not formed by Herbert Macaulay or by the duo of Macaulay and Azikiwe** as reported in other publications. In 1952, the **NCNC did not secure a majority in the Eastern House** of Assembly where the majority was rather held by independent legislators and if the 6 members of the **Ibadan Peoples Party (IPP)** had contested on the NCNC platform, the NCNC would still not have had the majority in the Western House of Assembly. There were **5** parties, ***not 3***, that participated in the Western Nigeria elections of 1951, namely: the NCNC, the Action Group, the IPP, the Otu Edo and the Ondo Improvement League parties. ***Eyo Ita was NOT a professor*** at all; **he did NOT leave the NCNC on his own** volition; **he did NOT "form" the NIP or the NYM** and **neither** was **his** own party. He was **never** the **Deputy National President** of the **NCNC!** There were **NO** national political parties *per se* formed in Nigeria before 1951; only activist organisations, whether or not called parties.

THE RISE OF POLITICAL ACTIVISM IN NIGERIA

Richard Sklar writes that "it was the destiny of Lagos, the leading port, administrative capital and commercial centre, to be the cradle of Nigeria's political party system as well. The rapidly growing number of settlers included many non-Nigerian Africans who, as a rule, did not readily identify their own interests with those of the indigenous Nigerians. Among them were, however, a number of journalists, barristers and other professionals who were involved in the early nationalistic political movements that were "African" first, "Lagosian" next and "Nigerian", as an afterthought."[8] Sir Udo Udoma also wrote that:

The Nigerian National Democratic Party (NNDP), which was formed on June 24, 1923 by Herbert Macaulay, Thomas Horatio Jackson and Bangan Benjamin for the purpose of contesting elections for the three seats granted to Lagos under the franchise introduced by Sir Hugh Clifford in 1921, functioned only in, and dominated the politics of, Lagos as a Crown Colony until it was challenged by the Nigerian (Lagos) Youth Movement.[1]

In 1934, the British colonial government created Yaba Higher College in order to train more Nigerian technicians. The college suffered for being a native Nigerian

Sir Hugh Clifford

institution, having no affiliation with any British university. According to the educated elite at the time, any college based in Africa was inherently inferior. Additionally, Yaba offered no courses on either public administration or economics, which were prerequisites for colonial administrative positions. The Lagos Youth Movement (LYM), founded by J. C. Vaughn, Ernest Ikoli, H. O. Davies, and Samuel Akinsanya [**not by Prof. Eyo Ita**] in 1934 and renamed the Nigerian Youth Movement (NYM) in 1936, according to *"Legacy: The Nigerian Youth Movement and the Rise of Ethnic Politics, 1934-1951"* by C.S. Momah and Hakeem Harunah[20], was created in protest of these inherently inferior educational opportunities. By and large, the traditionalistic predominantly moslem indigenous masses followed Macaulay and the NNDP while the Westernised traditionally Christian cosmopolitan (i.e., drawn from several provinces – Ijebu, Abeokuta, Oyo, Ondo and Lagos) rising class went with the NYM.[8]

POLITICAL PARTY vs. POLITICAL ACTIVISM

Wikepidea defines a political party as an organised group of people with at least roughly similar political aims and opinions, that seeks to influence public policy by **getting its candidates elected** to public office. Now, who is a political activist? *Reference.com* says:

> A political activist is someone who is involved in the political process for the sake of promoting, impeding or raising awareness of a certain issue or set of issues. Political activism typically involves engagement beyond just voting, whether it be through protest, demonstration or lecture.

Wikepidea adds that forms of activism range from writing letters to newspapers or to politicians, political campaigning, economic activism such as boycotts or preferentially patronising businesses, rallies, street marches, strikes, sitins, and hunger strikes. The bottom line is that if you cannot vote or are not allowed to vote, you cannot call yourselves a political party. Part of the problem is that Nigerians have a penchant for trying to run before we learn to crawl or even walk, no doubt exacerbated by western writers of African history not realising that colonized Africa was not a "free" people like them at the time.

Richard Sklar, for instance, wrote about the NCNC that:

> ... in emergent Africa under British and French rule, nationalistic pressures quickened the pace of constitutional advance which in turn stimulated the development of political parties. The classic Nigerian example is the Constitution of 1946 which gave an enormous if unintentional boost to the newly born NCNC. Largely as a result of intensive agitation by that party, a general review of the constitution was initiated by the government in 1948.[8]

If Sklar had writen "activism" in place of "parties" and "activist organisation" in place of "party", he would have been dead on the money! Prior to 1945, the groups that participated actively in influencing the membership of the legislative councils were all activist organisations because there was no open voting for such members by the populace as the legislative council nominees were chosen by the native authority, which consisted of expatriates. Even then, the limited franchise was 100 pounds which few people could afford in order to vote or be voted for. Even after the Richards Constitution came into effect in 1945 and regional houses of assembly were formed, those nominated into the regional houses of assembly and the legislative council were still so nominated by the native authority while the houses of assemblies could not make laws and were merely grounds for public discussion. The executive council in Lagos had Nigerians for the first time after the introduction of that Richards Constitution, in the persons of Adeyemo Alakija and S. Bankole Rhodes when the NNDP and the Nigerian Youth Movement (NYM) finally succeeded in getting the expatriate-laden native authority to do so, but only in Lagos. Also, while the constitution reduced the amount of the limited franchise to 50 pounds, thus allowing more people to vote and be voted for, it was still too expensive for most Nigerians. Sir Udo Udoma concludes:

> Otherwise, throughout the rest of Nigeria as a country, partisan politics was almost unknown until the entry of the NCNC as a national youth movement or political association, if you will.

Unlike Sklar, his mentor, James Smoot Coleman, was careful to describe activism in the west coast of Africa as **nationalism and political integration** because he knew the difference between what transpired and political party activities, and Richard Sklar, who finally published his book while lecturing at the University of Ibadan and later edited Coleman's "Nationalism and Developments in Africa: Selected Essays", should have known better.EN In the Appendix of his book, Coleman makes the conceptual distinction between a "nationalist movement" and "political parties". On the main difference between pre-war and post-war nationalism on the west coast of Africa, Coleman says[17]:

> ... in the former period, nationalism tended to be (as Lord Lugard insisted) the pasttime of the few educated minorities of Lagos, Accra, Freetown and Dakar; whereas in the latter period, these minorities, greatly expanded and dispersed to new urban centres in the interior, have made positive efforts to nationalise and popularise the crusade. ... the technique here has been (1). to make nationalism, and especially its objective of self-government, an integrating symbol in which even its most disparate goals could find identification; and (2) to **policitise** - one would like to say **nationalise** - all existing thoughts and associations.

FORMATION OF THE NCNC

The Nigerian Union of Students (N.U.S.) was another activist organisation inaugurated in March 1940 by students of Abeokuta Grammar School at the prompting of their principal, Revd I. O. Ransome-Kuti, founder of the Nigerian Union of Teachers. The N.U.S. soon evolved by merging with the students unions of other institutions like the Yaba Higher College and, together, agitated for political reforms for Nigeria and wrote to the Secretary of State for the Colonies with recommendations in the wake of each Nigerian constitutional conference. Because they were rebuffed each time, they took the initiative to forge a national front on the one hand, and also look into inviting established and respected nationalistic stalwarts to manage their movement and sign future submissions to the constitutional conferences in the hope that their recommendations would be taken more seriously. To those ends, the students' leaders decided that a central organisation was required to coordinate the political endeavours of social and political activism and earmarked certain patriots as future officers.

Richard Sklar wrote that the March 1944 King's College riot aroused both the ire of the Lagos intelligentsia and the latent militancy of the N.U.S.. On June 10, 1944, the N.U.S. convened a mass meeting at the Glover Memorial Hall to consider the King's College, Lagos strike, the raising of funds for a national school and the immediate formation of a representative national committee to be called the National Council of Nigeria (NCN). The venerable Herbert Macaulay was invited to chair the occasion. Resolutions were passed to set up the national committee and to look into the founding of a national college. These initiatives were pressed and over 40 organisations, including activist organisations, tribal and trade unions, literary and professional associations, religious and women's groups, and social clubs, were invited to attend the inaugural meeting of the National Council of Nigeria on August 26, 1944 under the chairmanship of Mr. Duse Mohamed Ali, an Egyptian who founded and edited the *Lagos Comet.* The then General Secretary of the N.U.S., Mr. C. O. Bamgboye, delivered the inaugural address, as reported by West African Pilot of August 29 & 30, 1944.[3]

Pursuant to its resolution to invite respected Nigerians to lead the National Council, they reached out to the doyen of Nigerian nationalism, Herbert Macaulay, to be their President.[8] Herbert Macaulay accepted the invitation with the proviso that his political son, Nnamdi Azikiwe, also came on board as Secretary-General. Coleman writes that, unfortunately, Dr. Akinola Maja, the President of the NYM and his associate, Oluwole Alakija, refused the subordinate offices of Vice President and legal adviser of the National Council, respectively.[3] By January 1945, the National Council comprised 87 member unions, including 3 Cameroon groups, thus necessitating the change of name to the *National Council of Nigeria and the Cameroons* (NCNC).[8]

It is not true that Macaulay and/or Azikiwe formed the NCNC and it is not true that the NCNC was a political party before 1951. **Nnamdi Azikiwe**, himself, wrote in his *My Odyssey* on page 303 that he only began to take an active interest in partisan politics in 1947 by standing for election to the Legislative Council and that he won the Lagos municipal election.[6] As we have just seen, he was the secretary-general of the NCN since 1944 and later Vice-president of the NCNC, and we know that he contested the Legislative council election on the platform of the NNDP in 1947 and not the NCNC. He also wrote that he spent 9 months in 1946 touring the whole of Nigeria and Southern Cameroon on a political (?) mission. Sir Udo Udoma wrote, as in the *Introduction* at page xii, that the NCNC successfully stormed the country, campaigning against the Richard's constitution and raising money to send a delegation of distinguished Nigerians to London to protest to Mr. Creech Jones, M.P., the then Secretary of State to the Colonies. That delegation, including Dr. Nnamdi Azikiwe, NCNC President and leader of the delegation, Dr. Ibiyinka Olorun-Nimbe, NCNC Treasurer, Prince Adeleke Adedoyin, NCNC General Secretary, Chief Nyong Essien, representing the Eastern Provinces, Mrs. Funmilayo Ransome-Kuti, representing the Western Provinces, Paul M. Kale, representing the Cameroons and Zanna Bukar Sulloma Dipcharima, representing the Northern Provinces, went on the mission and it should be noted that both Adedoyin and Olorun-Nimbe contended that the memorandum and conditional proposal submitted to Mr. Creech Jones on August 11, 1947 were drafted by Dr. Azikiwe alone[8]. Now, what was the end result of the mission described by Zik as political? In the continuation of the above passage, Sir Udo Udoma wrote:

> But Mr. Creech Jones, true to British tradition in respect to colonial administration of supporting outwardly the *raj* on the spot, right or wrong, turned down the petition of the Nigerian delegation. He merely advised the Nigerian leaders to return to Nigeria to cooperate with the British administration in working the constitution. That was in 1947.[1]

Azikiwe's reaction to the rebuff, as printed in West African Pilot of April 7, 1948, was that the Secretary of State for the Colonies *treated our national delegates and the national cause we sent them to present in a most summary, unpleasant, unfavourable and disappointing manner which we regard as a great insult to our entire nation*.[8] Now, why was Zik of Africa distancing himself from the delegation when he selected its members, he led it to London, as reported by Sklar[8] and acknowledged below by the NCNC Press Secretary in London, and he was the sole author of the delegation's submissions?

NCNC'S DEMANDS TO THE SECRETARY OF STATE

A press release was issued by Mr. George Padmore, the NCNC Press Secretary at 22 Cranleigh House, Cranleigh Street, London N.W. 1 in July or August 1947 for immediate publication. It announced that a pan-Nigerian delegation of seven people, under the auspices of the NCNC, arrived on July 10, 1947, charged by the people of Nigeria and the Cameroons to make the following demands of the Crown:

(1). To protest against the official policy of governing Nigeria and the Cameroons (which, in parts, are a Crown Colony, a Protectorate and a Mandated/Trust Territory) as if it were the exclusive colonial possession of Britain; and to ask for clarification of Anglo-Nigerian relations (a). in the light of treaty obligations and (b). in accordance with Protectorate status.

(2). To request repeal or modification of certain laws affecting possession of land, minerals and Chiefs of Nigeria and the Cameroons. These laws are inimical to their best interests and help to stultify their national aspirations.[16]

(3). To demand that immediate steps towards self governance for Nigeria and the British Cameroons be taken now.

What the NCNC did in that instance, as political and as patriotic as it may have been, is called *political agitation or, perhaps, activism* and not *getting their candidates elected* to public office!

NCNC DEFINED BY NCNC

Mr. Padmore's release laid out the names of all seven delegates, including Dr. Azikiwe, and the spirit of their mission. It also gave a definition for the National Council of Nigeria and the Cameroons:

The National Council of Nigeria and the Cameroons (N.C.N.C) is a federation of 183 political parties, trade unions, professional and business associations, tribal unions, youth leagues, farmers' and peasants' organisations, and other cultural societies all over Nigeria and the British Cameroons. **Its aims are political freedom, economic security, social equality and religious toleration.**[16]

A federation of such amorphous bodies as the NCNC claimed, including 182 other political parties in 1947 Nigeria, cannot be correctly described as a political party. Formed by students, the NCNC at that time was simply an activist body and was not concerned with legislative council membership nomination and, hence, was not a political party, as *per* its definition, by even *Wikepidea* itself. Clearly, agitating for **political freedom** is indicative of that freedom being non-existent.

Further, Dennis Chukude Osadebay said in his autobiography[14]:

... meetings gave birth to the National Council of Nigeria and the Cameroons as a United Front to fight against imperialism and for self-government. The NCNC was **not formed as a political party but as a supraorganisation** to which political parties, tribal and communal unions, trade unions and other bodies sent representatives.

Dennis Chukude Osadebay

See on pages 5-6 how, on the eve of the 1951 elections, thanks to the provisions of the MacPherson constitution, Azikiwe transformed the council, which was formed by Nigerian students who invited Macaulay and himself to join in, to a political party (as properly defined) without due consultation with the founders. Sir Udo Udoma wrote how later, as President of Ibibio State Union, he had the opportunity to speak to one of those students:

> Mr. D. U. Assam, in particular, explained almost in tears that he was one of the student founders of the N.C.N.C. as a national political movement in Lagos when a student at the then Yaba Higher College, Lagos and that it was a group of them, as students in Lagos, who had invited the late Herbert Macaulay of Kirsten Hall, Lagos, the acknowledged doyen of Nigerian nationalism, and Dr. Nnamdi Azikiwe, Editor-in-Chief of the West African Pilot newspaper to take over and manage the movement as a going concern as the General President and the General Secretary, respectively, which offices they both had gladly accepted. Further, he expressed astonishment at how, since the death of Herbert Macaulay, Dr. Nnamdi Azikiwe had taken over the movement and converted the same to a political party without any reference to the youth.[1]

ELECTIONS TO THE WESTERN HOUSE OF ASSEMBLY

In Part B, we see that after the elections to the Western House of Assembly, the NCNC won 24 seats, the IPP 6 seats and the AG 38 seats. Further, 3 AG secretaries contested the elections as independents making AG members in the house on the first day the assembly met **41, a clear majority**. If the IPP legislators had contested on the NCNC platform, the NCNC would only have had 30 seats. *Wikepidea* is lying.

ELECTIONS TO THE EASTERN HOUSE OF ASSEMBLY

Sir Udo Udoma is quoted on pages 8-9 as having written that:

... the majority of the candidates who were successful in the elections in the Eastern Region were not NCNC party supporters but independent candidates. Consequently, no effort was spared by NCNC supporters in persuading and prevailing upon the successful independent candidates to declare for, and join the NCNC party so as to enable the party to form the government in the Eastern Region, and also select the representatives of the Eastern Region for the House of Representatives, including members of the Council of Ministers in Lagos. ... Partly because of the appointment of Prof. Eyo Ita to head the government and partly for the unity of the region, the campaign to win supporters for the NCNC party in the Eastern Region was successful. In that way, the NCNC party was only able to form the government in the Eastern Region under the leadership of Eyo Ita.".

The Independent candidates that declared for the NCNC in the Eastern House included all 13 legislators from the British Cameroons.[18] The ***NCNC did not win majority votes in the East in 1951.***

PROFESSOR EYO ITA

1. Sir Udo Udoma gives us the following insight to how Nnamdi Azikiwe hoodwinked the world into thinking that his renowned columnist, Eyo Ita, was once a university don, leading to *wikipedia* hailing him as the "first Nigerian Professor".:

True or false, the story as told by Mr. Michael Ogon and repeated *ad nauseum* by other NCNC party supporters in the Eastern Regional House of Assembly during the debate (of no confidence in the ministers), was that, on arrival in Nigeria from the United States of America, Eyo Ita was the proud holder of degrees from 2 famous and distinguished universities, namely, B. A. (London) and M. A. (Columbia).

Dr. Nnamdi Azikiwe, who was then in Lagos as the Editor-in-Chief of the West African Pilot newspaper, being very impressed by such an academic achievement which was rare in those days, in his admiration he had extolled Eyo Ita to the sky and, in his enthusiasm, had described him as "Professor Eyo Ita". Thereafter, he had persisted in always describing Eyo Ita as "Professor Eyo Ita" in articles in the West African Pilot newspaper. ... He had adopted the practice of tagging unto all articles written by Eyo Ita and published in the West African Pilot the description "**by Professor Eyo Ita**", so that, by the process of autosuggestion based on the doctrine that a lie repeated often enough would come to be accepted as the truth, many people including Eyo Ita himself came, by the process of hallucination, to accept that Eyo Ita was a university don - a Professor who had held an academic chair in some university. Thus the title "Professor" became attached to the name Eyo Ita by usage and accretion.

If true, one can imagine at once that Eyo Ita was the victim of a mean commercial trick. For by the editor of a newspaper referring to a columnist as "Professor Eyo Ita", well knowing that the writer was not a "Professor" at all, and that he did not adopt the title "Professor" as a *nom de plume*, it becomes obvious that it was a device deliberately employed to boost the ego and reputation of the newspaper and thereby to increase its circulation. It was a trick perfected as a means of exploiting the ignorant masses of the people as, in those days, a high sounding university title was synonymous with wide knowledge and learning.[2]

2. Setting up the NIP was a natural reaction to the disenfranchisation of many members of the Eastern House of Assembly by Zik's civilian *coup d'état*. **Eyo Ita was sacked with ignominy and for life by Zik's NCNC wing.** According to Sir Udo Udoma, the new political party, having been promptly and duly formed at Enugu in February 1953, assumed the name of National Independence Party (NIP), which was suggested by Dr. Eni Njoku, Central Minister of Mines and Power. It had a large membership and included all the regional Ministers, except Michael Okpara, and all Eastern Regional members of the Council of Ministers who were central ministers, and who had all been sacked with ignominy and for life by Zik's NCNC wing, the core of whom founded the NCNC government. The leader of the new party (NIP) was, of course, Professor Eyo Ita.[1] **NIP was not formed by Eyo Ita, though, and it was not "his" party.** Sir Udo Udoma wrote that the NIP later merged with Alvan Ikoku's UNP to form the United Nigeria Independence Party (UNIP), which then became an organ of the Calabar Ogoja Rivers (COR) state movement, **the trail blazer.** It is noteworthy that after the voluntary merger of the United National Party with the National Independence Party, Dr. Udo Udoma was offered the post of the leadership of the UNIP, the new party thus formed, which he most humbly declined. But as a demonstration of the practice of self-effacement, a doctrine in which he most fervently believed, Dr. Udo Udoma had then in turn proposed Professor Eyo Ita, then already leader of the opposition in the Eastern Regional House of Assembly, to assume the leadership of the new party, which proposition was accepted but not without demur.

END NOTE (EN)

It is pertinent to note that **Richard Sklar** was 17 years old in 1947 when the NCNC leaders toured Nigeria. Thus, anything about that period, or prior, found in his book[8] (published in 1963 while lecturing at UI from 1963 to 1965 to memorialise his dissertation for completing his doctoral programme at Princeton University, USA in 1961), was gathered **second hand**.

A P P E N D I X   E

Prelude to the Foster-Sutton Inquiry

[Being an excerpt of the Address to the British House of Commons in July 1956 by the Secretary of State to the colonies, Mr. Allan Lennox-Boyd, captioned EASTERN REGION, NIGERIA (COMMISSION OF INQUIRY). A synopsis of events that led to the report is appended.]

"It is well enough that people of the nation do not understand our banking and monetary system, for if they did, I believe there would be a revolution before tomorrow morning."
~ Henry Ford

"With your permission, Mr. Speaker, and that of the House, I should like to make a statement, which is rather long.

A dispute has arisen in the Eastern Region of Nigeria about the relationship between the Premier, Dr. Azikiwe, and the African Continental Bank Limited. This Bank was founded by Dr. Azikiwe. On assuming office *the Premier informed the Governor that he had resigned his directorship of the bank.* He had enterprises *with* which he has been associated which are still shown as having large shareholders in it. I have been informed that during **1955, £877,000** of public money was invested in the Bank - and other large sums deposited along with it - out of funds made available from Marketing Board reserves to the Finance Corporation, which the Eastern Region Government had established.

Mr. Allan Lennox-Boyd
Secretary of State to the Colonies

I have also been informed that, following this investment, the bank was a party to certain documents contemplating that the Premier should be life Chairman of the bank and purporting to give him the right to nominate certain other directors.

As long ago as last November, I took the matter up with the Premier in London and we have been in correspondence since. In April of this year, Mr. Eyo, a member of the Regional House of Assembly, who had until then been the Government's Chief Whip in that House and Deputy-Speaker and Chairman of the Regional Development Corporation, tabled a Motion in the House relating to the association of the Premier with the Bank. He subsequently called for the appointment of an independent commission of inquiry. Dr. Azikiwe has now instituted libel actions against Mr. [E. O.] Eyo and certain newspapers.

On 14th July, after receiving a report from the Governor, Sir Clement Pleass, I sent a personal message through him inviting the Premier to agree to my appointing a commission of inquiry. I considered it essential that these matters should be fully cleared up before the next Nigerian Constitutional Conference. This Conference will consider further constitutional advance for Nigeria, and, in particular, the grant of regional self-government to those regions that desire it, in accordance with the undertaking given by Her Majesty's Government in 1953 as recorded in the London Conference Report.

I pointed out that such a commission was appointed in the United Kingdom when last the conduct of a Minister was called in question. I suggested that I should appoint the commission as at least one of the matters to be inquired into is reserved to the Federal Government and the Governor of the Region is not competent to appoint a commission to inquire into federal matters.

On 16th July, I **received from the Premier a message couched in terms which, I must confess, disappointed me**. His message, which has been quoted extensively in the Press, implied a rejection of my invitation. Shortly afterwards, I was informed that the Premier and his colleagues, after considering my message, **advised the Governor** of the Region to appoint a commission with a **sole commissioner of their own choosing.** Such a commissioner could not inquire into matters reserved to the Federal Government, of which banking is one.

On 18th July, I made a further approach to the Premier, explaining this again. I also said that, although it would not be proper for the Premier to suggest the full membership of the commission since he would be personally involved in its proceedings, I would nevertheless be prepared to invite the person whom he had proposed as sole commissioner to be a member of it. I said this as I was satisfied that the person proposed was suitable for appointment.

I regret to say that **the Premier rejected this second approach, also.** Instead, he and his colleagues now advised the Governor to appoint a committee of inquiry and nominated three persons to serve on it. Such a committee could not compel the attendance of witnesses or hear evidence on oath, and its investigations of matters reserved to the Federal Government would be of doubtful propriety. The Governor did not consider that to proceed in this way was, in the words of his Royal Instructions "in the interests of public faith" and informed the Ministers that he felt unable to act on their advice. This decision of the Governor, who has a most difficult and invidious task, has my unqualified support. In these circumstances, I have decided that in order to secure a speedy, impartial and full investigation as to the investments made in the bank, and the grave allegations that have been made - matters closely affecting the conduct of Government - it is necessary that I should now appoint a Commission of Inquiry. I have invited Sir Stafford Foster-Sutton, the Chief Justice of the Federation of Nigeria, to be Chairman, and he has accepted my invitation. The names of the other members and the terms of reference will be announced as soon as possible.

I earnestly hope that the Premier and his colleagues will accept the decision I have reached as in their own best interests and in the best interests of public life in Nigeria as a whole. I need hardly say that there is no question of any attempt on Her Majesty's Government's part to impose a British banking monopoly in Nigeria, or to dictate financial policy. The Commission will, I am sure, complete its work and report with all possible speed, but I am afraid that its appointment must almost inevitably mean some delay in convening the Constitutional Conference, which was to have met on 19th September. I hope that this will not be long, and I have asked the other Nigerian Governments to accept this delay, regrettable though it is to all of us, because in the interests of the Territory as a whole these serious allegations must first be fully investigated.

At the same time, I have made it clear to them that Her Majesty's Government stands by the undertaking given in 1953 about the grant of regional self-government to those regions that desire it. I trust that after the Commission has reported we shall be able to resume our work together."

Events that led to the Request for an Inquiry

In Chapter 9 of Sir Udo Udoma's constitution book[1], we find:

As previously indicated, the new 1954 Constitution of the Federation of Nigeria came into operation in law on October 1, 1954 throughout the country. On that day, the Eastern Region, like the other two regions of the North and West, achieved autonomy by the operation of law. Such autonomy entitled each of them to have its Leader of Government Business in the regional House of Assembly installed Premier of the region. In the Eastern House of Assembly, for instance, Dr. Nnamdi Azikiwe, leader of the NCNC and Leader of Government Business in the Eastern Regional House of Assembly, was promptly inaugurated Premier of the Eastern Region, while in the Northern and Western regions of the Federation of Nigeria, those inaugurated Premiers were, respectively, Alhaji (later Sir) Ahmadu Bello, the Sardauna of Sokoto, and Mr. (later Chief) Obafemi Awolowo. It was clear that federalism had come to stay.

... The Deputy Speaker [in the Eastern Regional House of Assembly] was **Mr. Effiong Okon Eyo** of Uyo Divisional Constituency. He was also appointed by the Premier as Chairman, Eastern Regional Production Development Board (later Eastern Regional Development Corporation) and Chief Whip of the NCNC in the regional House of Assembly. He became Deputy Speaker by election as a member of the Eastern Regional House of Assembly, having been **so nominated by the Premier**.

It may be a matter for wonderment that Mr. Effiong Okon Eyo should have been appointed and allowed to hold so many offices. For, as Chairman, Eastern Regional Development Corporation, he was allotted, free of charge, first class quarters formerly occupied by the expatriate officer who held the post before him and was also given a chauffeur-driven limousine. **His total emolument was reputed to be higher than that of the Premier of the region.** The reason for such an extraordinary situation was not far to seek. On presentation by the Premier in accordance with the promise made to him during the fight for the removal of Professor Eyo Ita as Leader of Government Business in the Eastern House of Assembly, **the Governor** had **refused to accept** Mr. Effiong Okon **Eyo for appointment** as Minister of Works in the Cabinet, because of the latter's antecedent history and record of having been to **prison for illegal circulation of counterfeit currencies**, when he was Native Administration Treasurer at the Uyo divisional administration. He had therefore to be appointed to the several offices by NCNC as recompense for his **past services to the party**.

[It should be noted that the Works portfolio was, as a consequence, given to Mazi Mbonu Ojike.] In continuation, Sir Udo wrote[1]:

... On assumption of office as Premier of the Eastern Region, to the astonishment of every one, Dr. Nnamdi Azikiwe requested that Ernest Odogwu Nwanolue Egbuna, Esq., Crown Counsel, be promoted Senior Crown Counsel in the Legal Department of the Crown because, according to him, provision had already been made in the "estimates" for that purpose. The Governor of the Eastern Region, Sir Clement Pleass, CMG refused to accede to the request, pointing out that, by law and the constitution, the civil service of the region, including the Legal Department of the Crown, had been insulated from politics and was within his exclusive control and jurisdiction. As a compromise, however, realising that the promotion was intended to be **in redemption of the Premier's election pledge made to the Obi of Onitsha,** the Governor released Ernest Odogwu Nwanolue Egbuna, Esq. from the civil service and agreed that he be offered the political appointment of the **Speaker of the regional House of Assembly,** charged with the **responsibility of controlling the proceedings of the House of Assembly.** That was agreed to by the Premier. And it was done so that, at last and in truth, "the stone which the builders rejected had become the head of the corner".

In the meantime, Mr. A. K. Blankson, then Manager of the West African Pilot, was appointed also Manager of the African Continental Bank, Limited with specific instructions in the handing over notes prepared by Dr. Nnamdi Azikiwe always to remember that Dr. Nnamdi Azikiwe's motive in founding the bank was **to establish a financial empire** thereby liberalising credit facilities in Nigeria.

... the 16 cannons of rectitude, which the Premier at his inauguration had pledged to observe as his guiding principles in the discharge of his high office, compared with the four creeds proclaimed by the Minister of Finance [in his budget speech], paled into insignificance and sounded somewhat pedestrian! The [Mbonu Ojike] speech, however, was well received by both sides of the House of Assembly. But, unhappily, it became the source of friction between the Minister of Finance and the Premier of the region. It was said that the Premier took strong exception to certain passages contained in the speech of the Minister of Finance.

Some of the passages to which the Premier objected were said to be:

1.   We believe in a socialist commonwealth;

2.   We are determined and have planned to finance those who meet the fundamental requirements;

3.   We are opposed to monopolies in any shape or form in our young but fast developing economy; and

4.   We must not be so recklessly ambitious as to commit financial suicide.

These, among other passages, were alleged to have been considered by the Premier as a veiled attack on his plan to direct investment of substantial government funds through the Finance Corporation, which was within the portfolio of the Minister of Finance, into the African Continental Bank Limited. To effect the investment was one of the urgent and "secret" duties already assigned to the Minister of Finance.

... After the inauguration of the Premier of the Eastern Region and the adjournment of the House of Assembly, it was announced with fanfare that Dr. Nnamdi Azikiwe, the Premier, accompanied only by Mr. L. P. Ojukwu, a well known business man and transporter as Adviser, was undertaking an Economic Mission to Europe and North America. The Premier did not take any Minister or Parliamentary Secretary with him, probably on the grounds of frugality. Moreover, there was issued no statement of government policy in relation to the overseas economic mission, nor any programme nor itinerary to be followed by the Premier and his sole Adviser.

On his return from the overseas mission, the Premier took time to prepare his report, which took the form of a booklet entitled: *A plan for the Rehabilitation of Eastern Nigeria*, the main purport of which was the advocacy of the investment of a substantial sum of money from the accumulated funds of the Eastern Nigeria Marketing Board by the Eastern Regional Government, of which he was Premier, as equity capital in the acquisition of the shares of the African Continental Bank Limited. **The names of the proprietors, directors and share holders of the bank were not disclosed.**

The booklet was nothing more than a piece of imaginative journalistic writing, involving the use of "weasel" words by way of propaganda in the process of **covering up a secret designed to divert public funds into a private bank**, registered as a private company, but **unlicensed in law** as a commercial bank under the Banking Ordinance of 1952. The economic mission itself turned out to have been an unsuccessful undertaking concerned with fishing out in the European market a possible pliable European agent willing to undertake the management of the African Continental Bank Limited, with the possible injection of government funds, during the absence of Dr. Nnamdi Azikiwe as Chairman, Board of Directors and Governing Director for life with the power to appoint other Directors. For, according to Dr. Nnamdi Azikiwe, having been appointed Premier, he had informed the Governor **that he had resigned from the bank.**

... The Eastern House of Assembly reassembled on 10th March 1955. The main business before the House of Assembly was to give consideration to the estimates of Revenue and Expenditure to be presented by the government and to pass the same into law. The estimates of Revenue and Expenditure for the whole of the financial year, being collectively known as the "Budget", the session of the Assembly was therefore known as the 'Budget Session.' It was usually the most important session of the House of Assembly in any given year. Without the House of Assembly meeting and passing the budget, the government would not have been provided with a Civil List, that is to say the government would not have been put in funds with which to run the affairs and manage the services of the region for the year.

As a general rule, therefore, the Eastern House of Assembly must meet at least once a year. What was peculiar about this particular assembly was that, for the first time ever in the history of the region, the budget was to be presented to the House of Assembly by a Nigerian Minister of

Finance, Mr. Mbonu Ojike - a well known nationalist [He was moved from the Ministry of Works to that of Finance after a cabinet reshuffle].

... At the opening of the meeting of the House of Assembly, following upon the usual practice and in the exercise of his discretion, the Governor addressed the House of Assembly. He delivered his address for the first time from the throne as a direct representative of Her Majesty, the Queen of Great Britain and Northern Ireland and head of the Commonwealth and also as head of the regional Government, being President of the Executive Council. In his address, the Governor dealt generally with the activities of, and policies formulated by, the Executive Council, alluding to the ministers collectively as 'my Ministers' and to the government as the 'Regional Government.' ... The Governor, however, ended the address on a personal note when he referred to the evils of bribery and corruption.:

No words from me are necessary to describe the evils of bribery and corruption, or their prevalence in this region, and Government is determined to do all it can to eradicate those evils. ...

Shortly afterwards, there ensued a battle between the Governor and the Premier of the Eastern region over what Azikiwe described as the decision of the executive council "to Nigerianise the civil service". According to Sir Udo Udoma[1], the Premier, who accused Mr. Lennox-Boyd of having acted in a clumsy and outrageous manner in support-ing the Governor, described the exercise of power by the Governor as untrammelled in consequence of which the Governor had lost the goodwill of the people of the region. Further, Sir Udo Udoma wrote[1]:

He (Azikiwe) concluded that the effect of the Governor's pyrrhic victory on the future of Anglo-Nigerian relations could not be assessed with exactitude, and, that it would be for the constitutional changes envisaged for the year 1956 to supply the answer. The Governor was described as a careerist, a bigot and an autocrat. The House of Assembly was then assured that, with the help of God, the Premier had pledged himself to resist with firmness the inroad which racial bigotry, careerism in the civil service and dictatorship was making into the region.

In all this, the Premier failed to mention that, even prior to the passing of the budget as presented by the Minister of Finance, the House of Ass-embly had passed a motion virtually abolishing the posts of provincial Residents in the debate of which members of the opposition had refused to participate. That motion was passed on 22nd March 1955 and had agg-ravated the anger of the Governor as it was openly supported by the gov-ernment. The motion, which was moved by the Deputy Speaker of the House of Assembly, the Chief Whip of the NCNC parliamentary party and Chairman of the Eastern Regional Development Corporation, Mr. E. O. Eyo, read **"that this house disapproves the policy of provincial administration and favours divisional administration and therefore** urges Government to abolish the existing system of provincial administration and set up machinery forthwith to administer all divisions in the Eastern Region directly from Enugu".

... Thus, the first political crisis deliberately precipitated by the NCNC government of the Eastern Region, under the leadership of Dr. Nnamdi Azikiwe, as a means of winning over Nigerian civil servants and rallying them round to the support of the government ended disastrously. The Governor of the region, with the constitution on his side all the way and the support of both the Colonial Office in Great Britain and the United Kingdom Parliament, achieved a resounding victory to the discomfiture of the Premier of the region and his Executive Council, who were worsted in the encounter.

In August 1955, the Eastern Regional government appointed a four-man commission of enquiry to investigate "the extent of bribery and corruption in all branches of public life within the region and to propose measures to remedy the evils found", which commission sat at different cities in the region from November 1955 to January 1956. One of two sensational cases they worked on involved allegations that the Minister of Lands & Surveys irregularly allocated urban plots while the other involved an allegation in November 1955 that the then Minister of Finance and Acting Premier (in the absence of Azikiwe in Europe), Mazi Mbonu Ojike, had corruptly awarded the contract of constructing the famous Onitsha market to an Italian building firm.

On the question of Ojike's guilt, the commission was divided - affirmed by Chuba Ikpeazu (the chairman) and E. E. Koofrey but denied by C. C. Mojekwu and J. A. Ita. However, the *Daily Times* newspaper of January 20, 1956, under the caption "Ojike Grossly Corrupted his office" published that the commission had found him guilty of misconduct. Azikiwe asked for his resignation the next day.[8]

With the above background in mind, we can now proceed to what precipitated the Secretary of State to the Colonies's request to the House of Commons for an inquiry. Sir Udo Udoma writes[1]:

... there developed an incomprehensible situation which could only appropriately by described as a cabal or triumvirate, consisting of Dr. **Nnamdi Azikiwe** as Premier, Mr. **Mbonu Ojike**, Minister of Finance with responsibility for the administration of the newly created Finance Corporation and Mr. **Effiong Okon Eyo**, Chief Whip of the NCNC party and Chairman, Eastern Regional Development Corporation, to rule the Eastern Region.

In 1955, on the eve of the visit to Nigeria of Her Majesty, Queen Elizabeth II of Great Britain and Northern Ireland and Head of the Commonwealth of Nations, the Premier of the Eastern Region dismissed Mr. Mbonu Ojike, as Minister of Finance and member of the Eastern Region

Executive Council, for having been **found guilty of corruption** by the "Ikpeazu Commission of Inquiry", which had been **set up by the Premier himself.**

Thereupon, in June 1956, after the Royal visit which took place in January 1956, Mr. Effiong Okon Eyo, feeling himself indispensable to the Premier, threatened that, unless Mr. Mbonu Ojike was reinstated in his post as Minister of Finance and member of the regional Executive Council by the Premier, Dr. Nnamdi Azikiwe, he himself would, in the month of August 1956, after the rendition of the accounts of his stewardship in respect of the affairs of the Eastern Regional Development Corporation, resign his post and offices in the NCNC party. This was absolutely uncalled for.

In his reaction to such a threat, the Premier without hesitation dismissed Mr. Effiong Okon Eyo as Chairman, Eastern Regional Development Corporation on the ground that the latter had lost interest in his important job of managing the development of the region. He ordered that his departure from the office should take immediate effect. Thus, the triumvirate collapsed like a pack of cards.

Since it was obvious that the Premier was peremptory in his order, Mr. Effiong Okon Eyo had no alternative but to pack up his bags and go away. But before his departure from Enugu, Mr. Effiong Okon Eyo raised an alarm. He proclaimed to the whole world, in a statement which he issued, that Dr. Nnamdi Azikiwe, as Premier, only dissolved the triumvirate, in a manner of speaking, because he had successfully, with the aid of members of the triumvirate, achieved his **greatest dishonest ambition** of diverting, by way of investment and deposits, public funds of the order of £2 million from the Eastern Region Marketing Board into the African Continental Bank, Ltd., which was founded by him and in which he had predominant interest. **It was in such circumstance that the African Continental Bank, Ltd. was able to obtain a licence to operate as a commercial bank.**

An accusation of that magnitude, which was highly and widely publicised, could not be ignored either by the Governor of the Eastern Region or by the Secretary of State for the Colonies in the United Kingdom. What was more, Dr. Nnamdi Azikiwe immediately denied the allegation. He went further to maintain that he had no knowledge that public funds of any kind had been invested in the African Continental Bank, Ltd. through the Finance Corporation as alleged. He threatened court action for libel, for heavy damages against anyone publishing the story.

... Thereupon, members of the UNIP opposition in the Eastern House of Assembly took up the matter. They petitioned both the Governor of the region and the Secretary of State for the Colonies in the United Kingdom on the matter, pointing out the seriousness of the allegation.

Fire on the Mountain!
~ By Theophilus Owolabi Shobowale Benson, *CFR, SAN*
*(2nd. Nigerian Federal Minister of Information -
Information, Culture and Broadcasting portfolio)*
~ *Ref: GUARDIAN of December 1, 2003*

*"No man's life, liberty or property are safe while the legislature is in
session."*. ~ Anonymous

Fire On The Mountain! was the signal chant for the political party war that erupted on the floor of the Western House of Assembly one bright morning in May 1962. The confusion and fracas in the House led the police to "tear gas" the chambers, which emptied within one minute as honourable members fled for their lives. That incident climaxed into the declaration of a state of emergency, following a motion tabled in the parliament by Prime Minister Abubakar Tafawa Balewa, on May 29, which was overwhelmingly adopted. Consequently, the Government at the centre declared a state of emergency in Western Nigeria for 6 months and Dr. Majekodunmi was appointed the administrator.

I was graphically reminded of that happening on the floor of the Western House of Assembly by the biography of Dr. Moses A. Majekodunmi titled "My Lord, What A Morning", which the Maye of Lagos autographed to me on August 30, 1998. This was after a meeting of some honorary titled Chiefs held at Chief Majekodunmi's No. 3, Kingsway Road mansion. Chapter 5 of the book from pages 140-180 dwelt on the Western Nigeria emergency. Dr. Majekodunmi, the administrator of the region during the emergency period, also retained his post as Federal Minister of Health. I feel a compulsion to tell the story of that political turmoil on the floor of the Western House for **posterity to know the truth** of the event. *I was the party general who strategised the NNDP/NCNC plan of action. All political parties played "political games and rascality" in those days* with the Action Group (AG) blazing the trail for others to follow.

I was in the chair at the party conclave, which *took the decision to confront and foil the Action Group in the House, should it be established through numbers that the party had oiled the NNDP-NCNC out of a majority in the House as it did in 1952.* But unfortunately, due to *over zealousness* on the part of the executors of the action, things were not carried out as originally planned.

In 1952, the Action Group propagated its philosophy of East for the East, North for the North and West for the West and argued that if an Hausa man could be leader of the government in the North, an Igbo man was leader of government in the East, then an Igbo man should not lead the government in the West. Of course, the Action Group philosophy gained ground. On its own part, the NCNC philosophy focused on *one Nigeria, one country and one constitution.* Therefore, the NCNC lost to the Action Group in the West. Even in the appointment of two of the five Lagos members to the Federal House, the Action Group voted against Zik in the Western House of Assembly, irrespective of the fact that NCNC won the five seats in Lagos. [??]

However, the man who led the East then (Eyo Ita), whom the Action Group regarded as an Igbo man, was an Efik and not Igbo. In its *"political game and rascality"*, the Action Group, *through vote buying and manipulation* had *vaporised the NCNC majority in the House* and this prevented Zik from being leader of government in the Western Region or going on from the West to the House of Representatives in Lagos. The Lagos Metropolis was then part of the West. At that time, members got to the Federal House from their regional Houses through Electoral College *except in Lagos where general election was conducted and the NCNC 'Five Men of Destiny' defeated the five members of the Action Group.* [Not true! p. 10]

The political imbroglio of 1962 centred on appointing a premier for the region after the *"sack me I sack you"* power play of the AG, which asked the Governor of Western Nigeria, Sir Adesoji Aderemi, to sack the Premier (Akintola). Adegbenro was nominated by the Governor to replace Akintola and Akintola fired back by sacking the Governor and later went to the High Court of Western Nigeria in Ibadan on Suit No. High Court (W.N) 1/16/62, claiming that he had been wrongfully removed. The High Court referred the constitutional questions involved to the Federal Supreme Court for decision and Akintola's claim was upheld by the Supreme Court presided over by Honourable Justice Adetokunbo Ademola, then the CJN, along with Justices Taylor and Bairamian, both Justices of the Supreme Court. Akintola went back to the High Court, which ruled in his favour, thereby upholding the dismissal of the Governor and also upholding Akintola as the Premier of Western Region. But Adegbenro appealed the judgement to the Privy Council in London and also brought an appeal to the Federal Supreme Court on Suit No F.S.C. 187/1962 from the judgement of the High Court. The Privy Council in London over-ruled the Supreme Court and gave judgement in favour of Adegbenro thus upholding the power of the Governor to sack the Premier and the appointment of Adegbenro as replacement for Akintola. The region was thrown into deep turmoil as there was no effective government and the parliament in Lagos had to step in to resolve the impasse. The parliament decided that, as a Sovereign State, the decision of the Supreme Court of the land was supreme and no further appeal in Nigeria would go to the Privy Council in London.

The Supreme Court had ordered that the Premier be confirmed by a vote in the House of Assembly to test the strength of the claimant factions. Both the rump of the AG and the NNDP claimed to have majority of Assemblymen, yet both parties wanted an alliance with the NCNC. *But remembering how Zik was spited and done out of his party's victory 10 years back*, the NCNC decided to team up with the Akintola and Ayo Rosiji's NNDP. Meanwhile, Chief Rosiji had been expelled from the AG for advocating an alliance with the North and the late S. G. Ikoku replaced him as General Secretary of the AG.

The NCNC strategy was to seize the opportunity of the all-iance to slap back the AG in the face to pay it back in its own coin for what it did to the NCNC in 1952 at the Western House of Ass-embly. [*We have seen that AG did nothing to NCNC.*] When the party learnt that the AG had enlisted an expatriate Greek business magnate and the National Bank to fund its **vote-collecting operation**, [*all in their imagination*] it fell on the NCNC to devise a method of blocking the AG. [*Why on NCNC and nobody else?*] *It was then imperative* *that the AG scheme for victory through manipulation and financial inducement be thwarted. Our counter political game plan was to seize the mace at the Assembly in order to nullify the day's session.*

On the D-day in the Western House of Assembly, AG and NNDP / NCNC alliance members each sat on opposite sides and galleries and each on the side of the seats where honourable members of their camp were to be based as they trooped into the Assembly Chambers. But **the NNDP/NCNC alliance was ready with the machinery it set up to stop and rubbish the AG. Riot police with guns and teargas canisters strapped to their waists were combat ready for any eventuality.** [True confessions!] As honourable members entered the Chambers, the Chief Whip of the NNDP/NCNC alliance counted them. The two candidates for the office were Chief Akintola for the NNDP/NCNC alliance and Chief D. S. Adegbenro for the Action Group. After the Speaker had entered the Chambers, **it became clear that the majority of members were on the side of the AG.** *To kick-start the operations, party whips gave the signal for action to Honourable Oke from Osun Constituency, as had been prearranged.*

He got up from the back row where he sat and jumping from one table to the other shouting repeatedly "Fire on the Mountain; Run, Run, Run!". He kept up the chant and the jumping exercise. Thus there was great confusion in the House as members packed their bags and baggage out of the Assembly chambers. The honourable member representing Ajeromi-Ajegunle Constituency, Mr. Ebube Dike, an Igbo settler from Okigwe, raced to the Speaker's table and made for the mace to hit it on the Speaker's head. The Speaker, Prince Adeleke Adedoyin, dodged it and the mace hit on the table and broke into pieces.

At this point, the confusion in the House knew no bounds as people ran helter-skelter, some bleeding from wounds. The police had thrown teargas canisters through the windows and the main door, hence people scrambled to flee through the ventilation holes of the Assembly. In the end, everybody managed to wriggle out of the Chambers and the police sealed off the Assembly. The state of emergency that followed foreclosed the Western House. [**To Zik's delight.**]

When Majekodunmi assumed duty as the Administrator, his first assignment was to detain parliamentarians; Awo in Lekki, Akintola in Olokemeji and some others placed under house arrest. When it reconvened six months later, Chief Akintola was restored to the

Premiership and Fani-Kayode was appointed the deputy Premier by Akintola. The office of deputy Premier was not in the constitution and I complained to Zik at the State House and also to Okpara but they asked me to meet Akintola to resolve the matter. Akintola's stand was to adopt any means to win the battle and one of them was to make Fani-Kayode the Deputy Premier. All the people who complained against Fani-Kayode were regarded as being jealous of him and we left the matter like that, thus Fani-Kayode was called "Fani The Power". That was the *kata-kata* that was going on in the Western House of Assembly before the army struck in January 1966.

In politics, when you plan one thing, your followers execute it wrongly. It was the assigned role of Ebube Dike to remove the mace, being the authority of the parliament but he attempted to hit the mace on the head of the Speaker. It was not the intention of NNDP/NCNC alliance that the mace be broken but only to remove the mace and end the day's session. Likewise, the instruction to Honourable Oke was to tap the table to arouse the attention of Ebube Dike and not to jump up and down, shouting "fire on the mountain!". However, Ebube Dike, in his ulterior motive regarded this as a reprisal action to pay back the AG on what they did to Zik in 1952, so 1952 remains a remarkable year for Igbos.

So the NCNC decided to punish Awo in 1964 when it reneged in a solid agreement to make Awo the Prime Minister. The 1964 elections saw the NPC victorious and Balewa was called upon to form the government at the centre but, instead of remaining with the UPGA (AG/NCNC Alliance), the NCNC joined the NPC to form the central government.**

** It should be noted that, on Sir Ahmadu Bello's directive, as NPC party President, Alhaji Abubakar Tafawa Balewa, the Prime Minister, invited the AG, the NCNC and the NEPU parties to join the victorious NPC in forming an all representative government at the centre, as Uncle TOS describes it, but Chief Obafemi Awolowo, leader of the AG, who had issues with Dr. Nnamdi Azikiwe, and Mallam Aminu Kano, leader of NEPU, who had his own issues with the Sadauna, turned down the offer, allowing the NCNC to fill half of the cabinet positions, instead of a quarter, and more importantly denying the government the vast experience of Awolowo, himself, who most likely would have been the Federal Minister of Finance. - the Author

"Carpet Crossing" Related Cases Lost by Zik Newspapers

> "A false witness shall not be unpunished, and he that
> speaketh lies shall not escape."
> ~ Proverbs 19:5

In Chapter XI - **Zik's Newspapers and the Law** - of Nnamdi Azikiwe's "My Odyssey"[6], we find on pages 342-343, under the caption "Enahoro *vs. Southern Nigeria Defender*", Dr. Nnamdi Azikiwe's the below synopses of the suit for libel that was instituted by the touted "first Carpet Crosser", Anthony Enahoro, against one of his newspapers. Mr. Justice Atanda Fatayi-Williams awarded Enahoro £1,000 plus costs.

And on pages 343-346, under the caption "Williams, Akintola and Awolowo *vs. West African Pilot*", Zik gives the following account of the suit that was instituted for damages against the newspaper for libels published in a series of catoons that graphically portrayed the plaintiffs as the "brain", "propagandist" and " Fuehrer", respectively of the "carpet crossing in the Western House of Assemby in 1952". The celebrated Justice Olujide Somolu ruled that "*... the publications complained of referred to the plaintiffs in a defamatory sense, and grave charges of fraud and other forms of dishonourable conduct had been levelled against them in those cartoons*". He, accordingly, awarded £10,500, plus costs, against the owners of the newspaper, an award Nnamdi Azikiwe described as the highest award of damages ever made by any court in Nigeria. He added on page 352 "That it was awarded by a jurist who had considerable experience as a working journalist demonstrates the nature of these libels." You would think that these two warnings would be more than *enough for the wise*.

ENAHORO VERSUS "SOUTHERN NIGERIA DEFENDER"

Chief Anthony Enahoro instituted legal proceedings at the Ibadan High Court against Associated Newspapers of Nigeria Limited (printers and publishers of the Southern Nigeria Defender) and S. N.

Iweanya, its editor, claiming £5,000 damages for libel contained in the issues of that newspaper on April 30, and May 1, 1959. The first issue contained a report of the proceedings of the Western House of Assembly and the second an editorial based entirely on the former.

The Plaintiff was represented by Chief Rotimi Williams and the senior Crown counsel (Mr. Eboh), while the defendants were represented by Babatunde Olowofoyeku. Inexplicably, the claim against the second defendant was discontinued by the Plaintiff before trial. Chief Enahoro maintained that the two publications were grossly inaccurate and that, consequently, he was defamed. The defendants set up pleas of **fair comment and qualified privilege**.

On December 1, 1960, Mr. Justice Fatayi-Williams delivered judgment on the case. He ruled that **for the plea of fair comment to succeed, the comment must be based on facts accurately stated**; and that since the **facts, as stated by the defendant, were grossly inaccurate**, that plea must fail. On the plea of qualified privilege, the judge maintained that for it to succeed, the defence must prove that the results of the parliamentary proceedings was fair and accurate and **was published *bona fide* and without malice**. In his opinion, however, since **the defendants had been reckless and had acted in utter disregard for accuracy**, this defence also failed.

Before awarding damages, Mr. Justice Fatayi-Williams took into consideration the fact that, in spite of the plaintiffs corrections of the facts, as reported on April 30, 1959, the defendants did not publish the correction. "Instead", he concluded, "a more serious attack, based on the same inaccuracies which they have made no effort to correct at any time, was launched on May 1, 1959. Bearing all this in mind, I award him £1, 000 damages with costs."[6]

WILLIAMS, AKINTOLA AND AWOLOWO VERSUS "WEST AFRICAN PILOT"

Chief Rotimi-Williams (Attorney-General and Minister of Justice of Western Nigeria), Chief Samuel Ladoke Akintola (Federal Minister of Communications and Deputy-Leader of the Action Group) and Chief Obafemi Awolowo (Premier of the Western Region and Leader of the Action Group) brought a consolidated action against the West African Pilot Limited (printers and publishers of the West African Pilot) and P. C. Agbu, its editor, claiming £30,000 pounds each, as damages for libels published against them in a series of cartoons with captions which referred to three principal characters as "the Brain", "the Propagandist" and "the Fuehrer", respectively.

They did not join the author of the cartoons; but when hearing began in the consolidated cases, on November 30, 1961, the plaintiffs withdrew against P. C. Agbu in each of their cases. He was thereupon struck out from the suits. It did not appear that he was ever served with the writ of summons. H. P. F. Milmo and Adenekan Ademola appeared for the plaintiffs and M. E. R. Okorodudu and R. A. Akinjide represented the defendants.

Each of the plaintiffs complained of various issues of the West African Pilot, to wit: (a). cartoon captioned "History of the A.G. No 8" appearing on page 4 of March 21, 1959; (b). cartoon captioned "History of the A.G. No 9" appearing at the right hand bottom corner of page 6 of the issue of April 4, 1959; (c). cartoon captioned "History of the A.G. No 10" appearing at the bottom of page 2 of the issue of April 7, 1959.

The Plaintiffs averred in their statement of claim that there was in 1951 a general election into the Western House of Assembly and that the principal political parties which contested the election were the Action Group (A.G.) and the National Council of Nigeria and the Cameroons (N.C.N.C.) and that A.G. formed the Government of the region after winning a majority in that election.

The *West African Pilot* was alleged to have published a series of the cartoons which were intended to deal and understood by the readers of the paper to deal with what happened at the 1951 election. The newspaper claimed, as purported by the cartoons, that it was the NCNC and not the Action Group that won the Western Nigeria elections of 1951 which is the brunt of the "Carpet Crossing" propaganda, and which has no basis in fact. The libels complained about were contained in various issues of the newspaper as follows: 1. cartoons that appeared on page 4 of March 21, 1959 captioned "History of the AG No. 8; 2. catoons that appeared on April 4, 1959 captioned "History of the AG No. 9; and 3. cartoons that appeared on April 7, 1959 captioned "History of the AG No. 10".

The plaintiffs also alleged that the person referred to as "the Fuehrer" was intended to be, and was understood by the readers of the paper to be the third plaintiff, Chief Obafemi Awolowo, who had been, and still was, the Leader of the A.G.; that the person described as "the Propagandist" was intended to be, and was understood by the readers of the paper to be the second plaintiff, Chief Samuel Ladoke Akintola; and the person referred to as "the Brain" was intended to be, and was understood by the readers of the paper to be the first plaintiff,

Chief Rotimi-Williams, who had been described in other issues and/ or other pages of the said paper as "the brain behind the Action Group" and "the brain behind the Government of the Western region."

Having referred to the action captions of the cartoons, the plaintiffs submitted that the publications meant, and were understood by the readers of the paper to mean that, prior to the 1951 election, the plaintiffs conspired to raise a colossal loan in order to win the said election by bribery; that at a top-secret meeting in 1951, the first plaintiff advocated that the A.G. party should employ people of disreputable character in order to win the said election by impersonation and fraud, and that he conspired with the other two plaintiffs to use such methods to win that election; that after an N.C.N.C. victory at the 1951 election, the plaintiffs conspired to bribe all waverers among the N.C.N.C. successful candidates so that they might join the A.G. and so give the latter party the required majority. These imputations were said to be false and, in consequence, the plaintiffs claimed to have been injured in their characters, etc.

"The Propagandist"
and "the Brain",
à *la* Zik Newspapers

The plaintiffs gave evidence on their own behalf and they confirmed one another's evidence that the cartoons referred to them. One witness testified for the plaintiffs but no witness was called by the defendants.

The defendants admitted the professions [submissions] of the plaintiffs in respect of the ownership of the *West African Pilot*, the general publication of the cartoons with their captions, the public offices held by the plaintiffs, but denied that the publications complained of were defamatory or were intended or understood to be defamatory by the readers of their paper. They raised the defence of fair comment and filed particulars in support of the same.

On December 22, 1961, Mr. Justice Olujide Somolu delivered judgment and held that the cartoons complained of were capable of referring to the plaintiffs, that having regard to the evidence of the plaintiffs and their witness, which the court accepted, it followed that the publications complained of referred to the plaintiffs in a defamatory sense, and that grave charges of fraud and other forms of dishonourable conduct had been levelled against them in those cartoons.

The judge ruled that the defence of fair comment required that the material facts on which the comment was based should be truly stated and that the subject should be a matter of public interest. In his opinion, as the cartoons contained only allegations of facts without any comment on them, the defence of fair comment was not available to the defendants. Even if this had been tenable, the fact that these libels were not contemperaneous with the events but were *a sudden crusade with no justifiable reasons to support it* would destroy the protection offered by that "rolled-up" plea.

Then Mr Justice Somolu maintained that once any publication had been found to be defamatory, the law presumed damage, but that in awarding damages the court was entitled to take account of all circumstances of the libel. He concluded: "Having given very careful consideration to all relevant factors in the case; having made all allowances in favour of the defendants that I possibly can; and having regard to the amount of injury which the character and reputation of the plaintiffs must have, or are likely to have, suffered as a result of these libels, I hereby award a total of £10,500 in their favour, i.e., £3,500 each, with costs which I shall now proceed to assess. Judgment for the plaintiffs."

This, Dr. Azikiwe wrote, was, incidentally, the highest award of damages ever made by any court in Nigeria as at that time.[6]

Dr. Nnamdi Azikiwe's Inordinate Ambition

"There is a loftier ambition than merely to stand high in the world. It is to stoop down and lift mankind a little higher." ~ American author
Henry Van Dyke

Azikiwe's Image before Politics

Nnamdi Azikiwe was never interested in the affairs of the Nigerian polity as a student in America. He never took any courses in any branch of government nor did he participate in any political or activist organisations as he used his chain of newspapers to later falsely promulgate. His only interest had been to amass wealth and his eventual involvement in politics was completely coincidental and not from any humanistic calling. He was, on the other hand, immersed in a cloud of suspicion for illegal activities up to when he returned to West Africa after his studies abroad and set up shop in Ghana instead of Nigeria, primarily because he was said to be the benefactor of his disciples, Mbonu Ojike and Nwafor Orizu, both of who were arrested for fraud a number of times, Ojike later dying as a result of stress sustained while going through the two tribunals that were set up, one resultant on, and the other on the heel of, his dismissal by Azikiwe from his post as Eastern Regional Minister of Finance. Because he was said to be the one who bailed each of them out of jail when arrested on suspicion of fraud, the two disciples were thought to be working for Zik. There are a number of later political stalwarts, like Alvan Ikoku and Louis Mbanefo, who avoided him because of his antecedents, as they were said to intimate. That Zik later used Mbonu Ojike to remove Eyo Ita from office, to fight the Ibibio State Union and to divert funds from the Marketing Board into his bank, ACB, on the one hand, and manoeuvred Nwafor Orizu into his position of President of the Senate on his promotion to that of Governor General, confirms their indisputable bond with him. Zik is said to have been driven out of Ghana as a result of his fraudulent deeds there. His modus operandus was to salvage the reputation of young men, like Orizu, Ojike and E. O. Eyo, who had fallen fowl of the law, so he could later use them as cat's paws for his own evil ends. Abyssinia Akweke Nwafor Orizu was so known

85

in America that he got write-ups published in *New Yorker* and the *New York Times* and an Australian UN employee in NY City wrote in his memoir, "What happened to the Ibo adventurer who called himself Prince Orizu?" In Sept. 1953, Orizu was convicted on 7 counts of 1950 fraud and theft of funds (>£32,000), intended to fund scholarships in the US, a case Zik was allegedly associated with, by default.24

On his way back to Nigeria, Zik saw, to his surprise, that there were a number of Africans in England who had, not only taken interest in the effects of colonisation around the world, but were actively involved with organisations like the West African Students Union, (WASU), and in the activities of the Labour party. A young Nigerian, Dr. Udo Udoma, for instance, had been elected as the first black President of a UK University Society while at Trinity College, Dublin and had fashioned his Presidential address at his installation as a critique of the colonial policy and especially of Lord Frederick Lugard's policy of Indirect Rule. When Lord Lugard received a copy of that address in pamphlet form and read it, the latter sought out this young man, met with him in London, shook his hand and requested his autograph on his copy of the address - a lesson it may be well for Nigeria's leaders to learn. That young man lectured Labour Party supporter groups and also joined with Mr. (later Dr.) Kwame Nkrumah, Mr. Jomo Kenyatta of Kenya, Dr. Banda of then Nyassaland and now Malawi, and Dr. Moody of London to arrange for the holding of Pan African Congress, which was to take place in Manchester in Aug. 1945. He was elected vice-president of WASU and editor-in-chief of WASU Magazine and chairman of its editorial board. He, in fact, hosted Kwame Nkrumah for 6 months when the latter first arrived in England and from the manner his humanity was reflected in articles by pundits, was enjoying the admiration of the British government and her citizens, the very people Azikiwe despised. Zik must have been elated to meet him; right?! The point here is that, like Nkrumah, Zik had a perfect opportunity to learn the intricacies of British governance, especially as it affected her colonies and his country, but didn't. Nkrumah did.

Zik's involvement in any type of activism only came about when Herbert Macaulay asked him to join him in assisting the Nigerian Union of Students in manifesting their programme of setting up a national union, the National Council of Nigeria. After Macaulay passed away, leaving him to carry the baby, he seized the opportunity that the MacPherson constitution accorded him to turn the council into a political party with which to use in raising the money he required to obtain an operating licence for his bank, African Continental Bank, Ltd. He contested the 1951 election from a Lagos constituency in the Western

Region and never campaigned anywhere else, not to talk of the Eastern Region. In 1951, parties were not required to be nationalistic in nature and the NCNC restricted most of its activities to the Western Region.

Protest to Creech Jones, M.P. & Eastern States Express

When, in 1947, the N.C.N.C activist organization continued its tour around the country after the burial of their President, Herbert Macaulay, Nnamdi Azikiwe stopped over at Aba to invite Dr. Udo Udoma, who he got acquainted with in London, as earlier intimated, to be part of a delegation of distinguished Nigerians that would go to London to protest to Mr. Creech Jones, M.P., then Secretary of State for the Colonies, against the enforcement of the Sir Arthur Richards Constitution. Though Udoma knew that the only reason Zik wanted him on the delegation was because he knew Creech Jones personally from his Labour Party days, he graciously declined but recommended a replacement, Nyong Essien, to represent the Calabar Province on the delegation. In 1949, Udoma received congratulatory messages from far and wide when he founded his newspaper, *Eastern States Express*, at Aba [Yes; complete with *Bad Man Kalabar!*EN5] As he wrote, "... Dr. Nnamdi Azikiwe ... failed to congratulate me on the occasion by reason of the fact, according to him, that I did not consult him before embarking upon the field of Journalism as a publisher and proprietor." The nerve! Udoma said that Azikiwe's reaction to his failure to consult him before embarking upon the project was to indicate to him that he was mistaken in his enterprise because it was likely that all his wealth realised from his lucrative practice in court, as an utter Barrister, would be wasted on newspaper publication, and that in any event, the newspaper was likely to expire within six months of its foundation. Udoma most humbly disclosed to him that, rather than allow the newspaper to be in liquidation within six months of its founding, he, Udoma, would be prepared to sell the last suit in his wardrobe to make sure that the newspaper survived. In other words, that he would prefer to be seen bankrupt to standing by and allowing his newspaper publishing company to go into liquidation. High and mighty *Zik of Africa* felt Ibibio people needed to obtain permission from him to spend their own money for the good of Igbos.

The Dissolution of the Western House of Assembly

Historians often document the *kata-kata* T. O. S. Benson relates (App. F) as follows: "*On Friday, May 25, 1962, a House of Assembly meeting called to debate a motion of confidence in the new government ended abruptly with a free-for-all fight involving the throwing of chairs. This caused the Prime Minister to call for a special session of the Federal Parliament for 29th May.*" We know that the Prime Minister tabled a motion at the special session to declare a state of emergency in the West, an otherwise peaceful region where people outside the chamber did not even know that anything was happening inside it on May 25, even though no such declaration of emergency had attended the rioting of a most severe nature in the Tiv Division of the North and the two incidents of widespread rioting in Okrika in the East when several lives and property were lost in each rioting. The motion was passed, despite Awolowo's vehement counter motion for amendment of Balewa's motion on the premise that it was *ultra vires* the constitution as related to section 65(3)(3) and above all, was uncalled for, unwarranted and a dangerous precedent. That evening, the Governor-General, Azikiwe, signed 13 Emergency Regulation Acts that gave effect to the state of emergency in the West. As Dr. Mobolaji Aluko intimates, "Western Region and Nigeria went downhill from there on, culminating in a military coup 3 years later that plunged Nigeria into a period of instability that we are yet to fully recover from, and justifying the idiom that, many a time, the road to hell is paved with good intentions."

Does my dear Uncle's near deathbed confession not give vent to Awolowo's declaration on May 29, 1962 that: "… the NCNC wants, naturally, to fish in troubled waters. If I were in their shoes, I would think that no occasion is more favourable than now to have a dissolution of the legislature of the Western Region …"? It behooves us all to carefully analyse Uncle TOS's interview and see how an ill-conceived prank, with Zik's footprint, led to later catastrophic consequences for Nigeria, and learn the lessons he has, by his gesture, challenged us to learn. Has not history belied his premise that "the NCNC philosophy focused on one Nigeria, one country and one constitution"? Even the party's secretary-general, Prince Adeleke Adedoyin, resigned from the party claiming "*the party's sudden clamour for three Nigerias instead of one*" as the reason why. [p. 43]. Well, is that not proof enough?

The Dissolution of the Eastern House of Assembly

We have seen that Azikiwe, who had ignored the East in his ambition to be the first Prime Minister of Nigeria and the richest man in Africa, proceeded to go and stage a civilian *coup d'état* in that region after losing out in the Western Region out of ignorance of the provisions of the MacPherson Constitution and failing to compel the NCNC central ministers to fuel his bank, ACB, with the Eastern Region's money in their trust in order for it to qualify for a license to transact business as a commercial bank. In Sir Udo Udoma's book, we find:

> It was mentioned further that the ministers did not raise objection but had insisted that they be supplied with copies of the latest audited accounts or balance sheet of the bank to enable them to determine the

position of the bank as regards "liquidity". Dr. Azikiwe refused to comply; despite repeated requests he had remained adamant. He refused to cooperate with the ministers. ... Zik's bank, that is the African Continental Bank Ltd. of which Dr. Nnamdi Azikiwe was founder, proprietor, Chairman, Board of Directors and Governing Director for life with the power to appoint other directors, was established as a commercial bank by Dr. Azikiwe in or about 1948, having converted it from a mortgage company which he had bought from John Idowu C. Taylor, Esq.

Consequently, the registrar of banks in 1952 refused to grant ACB a license and attempts to find partners for the bank in Britain failed because of its insolvency; hence Zik's *coup d'état.* He dethroned the then leader of government business in the East, Prof. Eyo Ita, because he was an "*mmong*EN2 man", and sacked from the NCNC, with ignominy and for life, the central ministers who had earlier asked him to produce his bank's papers for them to verify that it was solvent before lodging public funds in their trust into it and who refused to accede to his command to them to do so without the papers being produced because he, the party's president, said so - a short story; not long at all as Zik purported! He described their stance as "unwillingness to tow the (undefined) party line", "a crisis" and "an irregularity" in his "autobiography". The NCNC government in the East that he was *gung-ho*ing over was formed by these same people, most of who contested as independents and were won over to the NCNC to facilitate Eyo Ita becoming the leader of government business. Otherwise, there would have been no NCNC government for him to go and *gung-ho* over. The party at its inception was not an Eastern region party or an Igbo party though a good half of those who crossed carpet to ally with Eyo Ita and who were dismissed with ignomiry for life, like Alfred Nwapa, Enoch Oli, Reuben Ibekwe Uzomah and Eni Njoku, were Igbos.

Now, for the die hard Zikists-at-heart who are probably saying as they read this, "Well, it wasn't Zik's fault; he did not write the constitution!"; well, he in fact did! "***Nigerians themselves devised the new scheme!*** (p. xiv) and Zik attended both the conference in London and its conclusion at Ibadan. Also, be reminded that it was Azikiwe who, unsolicited, left Lagos to go to Enugu, where he did not belong, to engineer the activities that made it impossible to transact any business in the House without being put in jail. That apart, where in the democratic world does the same person take two bites of the same apple? **Zik was a sitting member of the Western House of Assembly which was in session at the time of the 1953 elections in the Eastern Region and therefore was barred by the MacPherson constitution from standing election a second time, anywhere. His election to the Eastern House of Assembly was *ultra vires* the constitution**

that he helped to devise. The same implied provision that stipulated that all the houses, both at the centre and at the regions, would run their normal course of 5 years, hence not providing for resignations or the separate dissolution of a house, a novice precedent (Nigerians always jump blindly), also cast Azikiwe's seat in the Western House in stone for 5 years, barring its dissolution, **since that restriction was not changed**! As a reminder, the resignation Prince Adedoyin tendered to leave Parliament was not accepted and none of the alleged resignations during Zik's civilian *coup d'état* attempt was considered.

These suspicious activities should raise eye brows because the Igbo nation has been crying for decades how the colonial government favoured the North over the others (of course, to Igbo nation it alone constitutes "the others"). But both Governors of the Eastern Region during the period of Zik's foray into the region, Sirs Clement Pleass and Robert Stapledon, both connived with Zik in carrying out his evil plans. First and foremost, Pleass dissolved the House of Assembly rather than deal with the Ibadan renegade causing the impasse in the House. The fact that the naïve members of the House of Representatives gave the Deputy Governor the option to dissolve the House but did not give such a dissolution option to the House of Representatives if a similar event as occurred in the Eastern House were to occur in Parliament, says it all. Secondly, he then allowed Zik to contest election to the House, even though a member of the Western House! Then when Zik was found guilty of abuse of office by the Foster Sutton enquiry, Stapledon did not have him indicted and tried for the crime. And yet, the colonial masters were favouring only the Northerners? What did they even do in favour of the North, please? Instead, it was Colonel Frederick Lugard who, in 1900 as the new High Commissioner appointed by the Colonial Office discovered that the British Protectorate of Northern Nigeria was only on paper as there was no evidence of effective occupation as stipulated by the West Africa Act of 1885 and raised an alarm - the exact opposite of the claims of Igbo nation. They also keep talking about the coalition of the NPC and NCNC parties with Zik not having any powers, without even knowing what a coalition government really means? Do you have a coalition after decisive elections? Do you have powers after losing the election?

Only in Zik's books. He did the same thing after the Western Nigeria elections of 1951, when he appealed to Awolowo after his party had "lost" the elections to the Action Group, for a coalition and one of his own editors, Anthony Enahoro, called him out (pp. 16-17). In a proper coalition of parties, as with that of AG and NCNC that T. O. S. Benson alludes to in Appendix F, only one candidate is put forward for elections by the coalition, the other steps down, which is the main reason for a coalition of parties before elections. You don't contest election for Premier or Prime Minister and then ask for a coalition after you have lost in the election and then use your chain of newspapers to hoodwink the world about what is going on (*cunny-cunny*ᴇɴɪ). Now, in the case of "coalition government", which is a form of government in which political parties cooperate to form a party, the usual reason for such an arrangement is that no single party achieved an absolute majority. The only other times a coalition government may be desirable is in a time of national difficulty or crisis, none of which applied to the independence or republican election. Sirs Ahmadu Bello and Abubakar Tafawa Balewa, in spite of resounding victory at the polls and the constitution empowering the NPC to set up the government, invited, in the spirit of collective cooperation, the other parties to join in forming an all representative new government (completely from the goodness of their hearts) and only Zik, no surprise, jumped on board. Awolowo and Aminu Kano refused to join because of their respective grudges with Azikiwe and Ahmadu Bello. In fact, to prove that the government was not even only an NCNC-NPC government, K. O. Mbadiwe, who contested the election as his own party's candidate [the author forgets the name and has been trying, in vain, to reach Greg "*ihe Mazi Ozumba choro*" Mbadiwe to find out. But the motto of his party was "Forward ever, backward never".] as a result of his quarrel with Azikiwe, who was accusing him of plotting to have him assassinated, which Arondizuogu elders can corroborate. But both NPC leaders liked and got along with Ozumba Mbadiwe and were happy to have him. Yes, the government was and still is referred to as a coalition government but that again is the result of another Nigerian foible which is to want to run before we learn to crawl, not to talk of walk. Nigeria desperately has to start a program to indoctrinate the society with constitutional awareness, the lack of which partly derailed Zik's "*cunny-cunny*ᴇɴɪ" forays. He was devoid of constitution savvy or acumen.

After usurping the leadership of the Eastern Region by intimidation, eleventh hour *Igbo affinity* and hoodwinking publications by his chain of newspapers, claiming to be "regularising the irregularity", **Zik lied** to the Governor, Sir Clement Pleass, that he had resigned his directorship of African Continental Bank (ACB) in order to serve as Premier of the region. Under the code of conduct for ministers, a government officer was required to relinquish his holdings in private business to be eligible to assume public office. On assumption of office as Premier, did Azikiwe not then appoint his long time soldier, Mbonu Ojike, who Richard L. Sklar confirms was instrumental in the overthrow of the Eyo Ita Government in 1953", as Minister of Finance, and assign him the urgent and "secret" duty of directing investment of substantial government funds through the Finance Corporation, which was within his portfolio, into ACB from the region's Marketing Board for the purpose of obtaining, for it, an operating commercial license? (App. E)

The Three Musketeers in Action

Zik's attempt to also have the Governor accede to his request that Ernest O. N. Egbuna, Esq., Crown Counsel, be promoted Senior Crown Counsel in the Legal Department of the Crown because, according to him, provision had already been made in the "estimates" for that purpose, failed. Egbuna had been vilified in 1944 by Zik's group of newspapers for supporting the new constitutional proposals introduced by the then Governor of Nigeria, Sir Arthur Richards, which resulted in her regionalisation into three units of the North, the West

Mazi Mbonu Ojike

and the East, granting her Legislative Council for the first time full jurisdiction to legislate for the whole of Nigeria, which scurrilous press attack resulted in Egbuna being ostracised by his Onitsha people and by litigants, including some of his clients, and subsequently he abandoning his once very lucrative practice. So, no doubt, Egbuna was now to be brought in as Zik's "God forbid" advocate in the event that his secret plan imploded and he got indicted, as was nearly the case. "**God forbid** a tribunal gets set up and I am found liable, it will be incumbent upon the Senior Crown's Counsel to prosecute me. The *quid pro quo* understanding we now have, thanks to the Obi of Onitsha mediating, will preclude Egbuna from doing so." as was the case with the Senior Crown counsel in office during the Foster-Sutton tribunal.

The Premier's attempt to bring the fourth *Musketeer* into his cabinet also failed. Sir Udo Udoma writes that "the Governor had refused to accept Mr. E. O. Eyo for appointment as Minister of Works in the Cabinet, because of the latter's antecedent history and record of having been to prison for illegal circulation of counterfeit currencies, when he was Native Administration Treasurer at the Uyo divisional administration. He had therefore to be appointed to several offices by

NCNC as recompense." So the cabal or triumvirate that then ruled the Eastern Region consisted of the ***Three Musketeers*** that orchestrated Eyo Ita's exit from office - Azikiwe, Ojike and Eyo. Further:

> It was known that the Premier was never enamoured by expatriate civil servants. The impression also gained ground that he had always regarded them with suspicion. Such an attitude on his part, perhaps, had prompted him to employ a Nigerian Legal Adviser, personal to himself, whose advice he apparently relied upon in preference to the advice of a whole galaxy of the establishment of the government legal department comprising expatriate and Nigerian officers, placed at his disposal and at the head of which there was an expatriate of considerable experience and skill. ... It was obvious that all was not well with the Governor's Executive Council. There had occurred a serious question of policy differences of opinion between the Governor, on the one hand, and the Premier and his fellow ministers of the government, on the other hand. The dispute was in connection with the public service of the region.

The Governor had earlier referred to the evils of bribery and corruption in his maiden address to the Assembly. Shortly after that, the first political crisis deliberately precipitated by the NCNC government of the Eastern Region, under the leadership of Azikiwe, as a means of winning over Nigerian civil servants and rallying them round to the support of the government ended disastrously. (App. E)

As Sir Udo Udoma annotated, a thorough examination of the relevant provisions of the constitution makes it abundantly clear that the Governor was solely responsible, subject only to any directions issued by the Secretary of State for the Colonies, for the attendant policy. Under Section 175 of the constitution, whereas the regional Commission was bound to advise the Governor, the latter, even when so advised, was not bound to act in accordance with such advice. Thus, the claim by the Premier that the Governor was bound to act in accordance with the advice of the Executive Council was undoubtedly ill-founded because **a written constitution does not admit or recognise the existence of any convention.** By attempting to force or compel the Governor to act contrary to his own discretion but in accordance with the advice of the Executive Council, the Premier was, not only compelling the Governor to commit an illegality or to act unconstitutionally, but was trying to **usurp** the functions properly vested in the Governor. It was therefore wrong, constitutionally, but also unfair and unjust for the Premier to have accused the Governor of absolutism for which, according to the Premier, the former deserved "the fate which had befallen the Stuart King who was beheaded as a tyrant". How ironic!

On 5th April 1955, the Speaker received a letter dated that day and addressed to him by the Governor requesting him to introduce into the House of Assembly another bill prepared by the Governor for the purpose of restoring to the *status quo ante* all the provisions of the estimates of expenditure whether reduced, deleted or downgraded.

This bill is introduced to the house by the Governor under the provisions of Section 67 of the Nigeria Constitution Order in Council 1954.

The House, having adjourned *sine die* on 29th March 1955, the Speaker, the *unfrocked Musketeer*, Ernest Egbuna, had to summon another meeting of the House to be able to introduce the bill and have it passed into law within the stipulated time. Accordingly, the House reassembled on 19th April 1955. Acting on the direction of the Speaker, the bill was laid on the table of the House by the Clerk. That action on the part of the Clerk of the House was greeted with silence by the whole Assembly. There was no response even when the Speaker put the question "Second reading, what day?" Thereupon, the bill was deemed to have passed into law. So, because Zik had succeeded in toppling the government and enthroning himself Messiah in the Eastern Region, basically by running roughshod over anyone who got in the way, he figured "why not adopt the same tactic with the new governor that I did with his predecessor and got my way?" Well, Governor Pleass

proved to be a punching bag that punched back and won by **KO**!!

Also, see in Appendix E how, despite the verdict of the Ikpeazu Commission Zik set up to investigate corruption in the region being split on Ojike's guilt, he forced his long-time devoted soldier out of his government, dismissing him on the eve of the visit to Nigeria of Her Majesty, Queen Elizabeth II of Great Britain and Northern Ireland and Head of the Commonwealth of Nations and how, Eyo seeing what had transpired between the two *Musketeers* and "... feeling himself indispensable to the Premier, threatened that, unless Ojike was reinstated in his post as Minister of Finance

Her Majesty,
Queen Elizabeth II

and Executive Council member, he himself would resign his posts in the NCNC party and government. [Which was utterly uncalled for.]

The Premier without hesitation dismissed Eyo as Chairman, ERDC on the ground that the latter had lost interest in his important job of managing the development of the region. He ordered that his departure from the office should take immediate effect. **Thus, the triumvirate collapsed like a pack of cards**." and E. O. Eyo, then left out in the cold, decided to expose the Premier's crime by tabling a motion in the Eastern House of Assembly, calling upon the Governor of the region, Sir Clement Pleass, to set up a Commission of Inquiry to enquire into the circumstances in which substantial money belonging to the Marketing Board was invested in ACB, founded by the Premier, Azikiwe. He, his family, and the Zik Group of Companies were the principal shareholders of ACB which later (with Festus Okotie-Eboh appropriately instated as Finance Minister to ensure compliance) loaned over £163,000 to the Group at low interest, which loans the Group did not have to refund until 1971, thus distressing the bank!

Should the Senior Crown Counsel of the region, as a presumed patriot, not have prosecuted him for corruption using the report of the tribunal as probable cause, rather than break his oath and not do so, for "solidarity" [*igbo affinity*] reason? Here's the Governor's take:

> *The exercise of public power for private profit is established in the East.* The aim of the colonial government was not to establish a standard of honesty in public life; only time and education can do that. ... A number of sensible people realised that *Zik had done harm in the East in the last two years,* but the mass of the people, ignorant and uneducated, voted him back to power.

They voted him back because he was not prosecuted and half of those so-called uneducated people were not made aware that any wrong doing had transpired or that he was contesting unconstitutionally each time he contested. But you, Governor, knew; if he had been prosecuted, he wouldn't have been eligible to contest at all. You did not prosecute because you wanted him to be able to contest again, just the same way your office allowed him to contest the first time; period! In the meantime, those people you are blaming for your pretended inability to do anything about the situation are telling the world how you people are favouring the North to their detriment. You don't realise that your predecessor already told us that, according to the constitution, the legal department is within your exclusive preserve.]

The above statement by Her Majesty's representative in the East was a complete **cop out**. The Legal Department of the Crown was within his exclusive control and jurisdiction. Which British politician, found guilty of such impropriety, by a high profile tribunal, would be allowed, not only to go scot-free, but also to contest election to return to the office he disgraced, especially if he was not even eligible to be in office the first time? Where is the record of the returns from the money

Zik ordered to be so illegally "invested"? The British were so bent on chasing their humbug from Lagos to his kit and kin that they did not care what he did there once he got to them! Suffice it to note, as Prof. Coleman intimates, that nationalism, the quest for self-government, in Nigeria, is as much *a fulfilment as a failure* of British policy.

Now, without apologising to Ojike, who indeed facilitated his grave impropriety of **investing government money in his private bank**, ACB, did Zik not go on to become Nigeria's Senate President, Governor-General and then President undeterred? His dejected loyal soldier, Ojike, died at 42 years old, barely 2 weeks after the tribunal ended, of hypertension caused by all the stress he endured. Zik never atoned for facilitating events that led to the dissolution of the legislatures of both the Western and the Eastern Regions, either. Go figure!

Nnamdi Azikiwe vs. Ibibio State Union and *"mmong*[EN2] *people"*

Ndi igbo may be wondering why their revered "leader of Nigeria who was not, thanks to *mmong* people" as 'Henry, the igbo entertainer' used to sing, appointed E. O. Eyo to multiple offices and allowed him to earn more than the Premier himself? Well, he had to be compensated for doing the heavy lifting of Zik's attack on the Ibibio State Union and the COR State movement that the Premier thought were in his way of achieving his ambitions, as already stated. Thanks to his agents like Ibanga Akpabio, the uncle of Godswill Akpabio, Udo Adiaha Attah, the father of Obong Victor Attah and E. O. Eyo, who were *mmong* people themselves, he was able to wage those wars remotely. Akpabio and Attah were two of the five students awarded scholarships by the Ibibio Union in 1938 to go abroad to any University of their choice to study any professional course of their choosing, with the understanding that on their return, they would refund to the Union, by monthly instalments, the cost expended on their behalf by the Union, with which funds other Ibibio students could be sponsored. On their return, Azikiwe co-opted them to embarrass and antagonise the Union, their benefactor. They both refused to pay back to the Union the amount of money spent on their behalf, heeding Zik's advice. Also:

Ibanga Akpabio: who studied Education was appointed Principal of the Ibibio State College, a secondary school located in Ikot Ekpene, Akpabio's home town, freshly founded by the Union. It was the duty of Akpabio to see to it that approval was obtained for the commencement of the school. That, he failed to do. No step was taken by Akpabio to form contact with the Department of Education (DOE). The pages of the West African Pilot became the only means of communication with the DOE, Calabar and, indeed, the only means whereby Akpabio had chosen to ventilate his feelings against the DOE and the

Colonial Government. There was a complete impasse between Akpabio and the DOE, apparently ostensibly to the delight of Nnamdi Azikiwe. The Union had to wait for Dr. Udo Udoma to return and a delegation led by him to the Ministry to immediately resolve the impasse and obtain the required approval to allow classes to finally start.

Next, Akpabio decided, on Azikiwe's bidding, to go into politics without obtaining dispensation from his employers, the Ibibio Union. Having been elected to become a member of the two Houses of Legislature in the country, it became quite clear that Mr. Akpabio had chosen for himself an entirely new career as a full-time politician, being a full-time member of Parliament. His new status, as such, was incompatible with his continuing in his previous office as Principal, an office requiring full time employment, complete dedication and devotion. The situation was so embarrassing to most Ibibio people, that, curiously enough, it was the people of his own Ikot Ekpene District of the union who were the first to register a protest as to the anomaly thus created.

As if that was not bad enough, in 1950, as a result of the commission of inquiry which was set up by the Union and conducted by Mr. E. O. Inyang, it was discovered that, whereas Akpabio was appointed Principal, lbibio State College, lkot Ekpene at a salary of £360 per annum, he had, in abuse of his office, placed himself on a salary of £540 per annum without the knowledge, approval, and authority of the Union [just like his nephew and his NASS colleagues, under David Mark did]. The high handed manner in which this was done by Akpabio caused great discontent among members of the junior staff of the college. Senior students in the college were vociferous in their complaints about lessons missed because of the absence of the Principal. Class masters agitated against being overworked and having to teach extra subjects and extra classes. Some masters threatened to refuse to take on extra classes or to accept extra responsibilities without adequate remuneration. Some masters were quick to point out that it was unfair for Akpabio to still retain his post in the college as Principal, for which he was still receiving salary while rendering no service in return. What was worse, he was also being paid by Government as a member of both the Eastern House at Enugu and the Federal House of Representatives at Lagos in addition to whatever perks members of both Houses of Legislatures usually received.

Many important members of the union, Ikot Ekpene District complained bitterly of being embarrassed by the activities of Akpabio. Some of the people felt slighted because Akpabio would not listen to the advice freely proffered to him. Many of his supporters even felt disappointed by the extraordinary manner in which he was conducting himself since he won the general elections. They complained that he had taken to smoking cigarettes, a newly acquired habit! They had advised him not to seek election at Enugu to the Federal House of Representatives but to no avail. Representations were made by special delegations from Ikot Ekpene District to the offices of both the National President and the First National Vice President, Mr. R. U. Umoinyang. Despite receiving a letter soliciting his cooperation, Akpabio refused to cooperate with the Special Committee. He was firmly unwilling even to produce any of the books for auditing by members of the committee on the ground that he was not under any obligation to render account of the finances of the College to the Union because the bulk of the funds yielded as revenue to the college had been derived from school fees, all of which had already been spent on the college by him. Such was considered an extraordinary attitude to be adopted by Akpabio, as Principal, but Azikiwe was basking in euphoria, loving it all!

Then on 16 April, 1952, the union's National President, by his letter of that date which was addressed to and served on Ibanga Akpabio, suspended the latter from his office as Principal of the college. Despite that letter, Akpabio continued to employ himself in the college as Principal and regularly paid himself his normal salaries and other emoluments as if he was still teaching full time in the college. This attitude on the part of Akpabio caused considerable resentment. The impression was created that the Union, as proprietor of the Ibibio State College, was as powerless to bite as a toothless bulldog. Rumours then took the field that Akpabio was claiming the college as his personal property from which the Union was not entitled in law to dislodge him. It was well known that he was already in close communication with Azikiwe. Mr. Akpabio considered it his duty to keep Azikiwe informed of the affairs of both the College and the Union. Realising that he had no support in both Ikot Ekpene and Abak Districts of Ibibio State in his new venture of snatching the College from the Union, its founder, proprietor and financier, Akpabio seized the opportunity of his regular visits to Lagos as a Member of the Federal House to woo a group of persons of Ikot Ekpene and Abak extraction resident in Lagos and to solicit their help. And it was not denied him.

Akpabio, thereafter, threw himself wholly, as it were, into public affairs in relation to his membership of both the Eastern House and the Federal House. He had also to attend to his constituency duties. Thus engaged, his absence from the college was seriously felt. Complaints began to pour galore into the National Secretariat, Uyo, and the Chambers of the National President. His prolonged absence from the college also became a source of great anxiety to the Union. As a result of such absence, the students entrusted to his care were exposed to hardship, suffering and indiscipline for want of supervision because, as Principal in charge of a mixed college of boys and girls, he was placed in *loco parentis* to the students. Having failed to win for the college recognition and approval for the Post Primary School Leaving Certificate Examinations and grants-in-aid by Government, despite enormous sums of money spent on the college by the Ibibio State Union for over six years since the college was founded in 1946, Akpabio's continued attachment to the school was counter productive.

It was common knowledge that, as Principal of the College, Akpabio was almost habitually at daggers drawn with the DOE of the Eastern Region of Nigeria. He always treated with disrespect any inspection report issued on the College by Government Inspectors of Education. In 1949, Mr. A. H. Parnaby and Mr. N. C. Kay of the DOE inspected the College, and as was their duty, issued an official inspection report which turned out to be critical of the college. Instead of referring the report to the Union, as the proprietor of the college, Akpabio reacted in a most extraordinary manner. He wrote a most insulting and abusive letter to the DOE, Enugu, to which he also returned the critical report without the knowledge and consent of and, indeed, without any reference to the Union. When later the situation was brought to the notice of the Union by the DOE, the request by the Union that the abusive letter be withdrawn as likely to damage the reputation of the College was calculatedly ignored by Akpabio.

It also came to light that, during the formation of the government in Enugu, Eastern Region of Nigeria, Akpabio had freely offered his name for appointment as a Regional Minister of Education. His name was rejected by the Lieutenant-Governor because of the opposition, it was claimed, demonstrated by the Civil Service establishment under the leadership of Mr. C. T. Quin-Young, then tipped as likely to be appointed Permanent Secretary, Ministry of Education, Eastern Region of Nigeria. Mr. C. T. Quin-Young was, for many years, Provincial Education Officer and later Chief Inspector of Education in the East. Akpabio thenceforth began openly to lay claim to the College. He first asserted that he was acting as a representative of the Annang section of the Union in claiming the ownership of the college for the simple reason that the college was sited at Ikot Ekpene on a piece of land belonging to Annang people. The claim was immediately repudiated by leading Annang personalities both in Abak and Ikot Ekpene.

Akpabio was taken to court and his benefactor immediately sent him two lawyers to defend him, an expatriate lawyer named McCormack and an Igbo lawyer named Obianwu. After devastating evidence by Mr. Robert Udo Umoinyang, as the First National Vice-President, supported by tendered documents in court, Mr. McCormack, Counsel for the defendant, withdrew from the case in disgust during a short adjournment. Azikiwe and Akpabio had lied to him. The baby then had to be carried by Mr. Obianwu, his junior. On resumption, Mr. Obianwu applied to the court for adjournment on the ground that he had advised his client, Mr. Akpabio, in his own interest to have the matter settled amicably out of court. Mr. Obianwu observed that Mr. Akpabio had realised after his discussion with him that he had made a mistake in seeking to claim the college as his private property. Who does that kind of thing?! Mr. Obianwu then appealed to Dr. E. Udo Udoma, counsel for the Ibibio State Union, to agree that the matter be settled out of court as a means of effecting reconciliation. Dr. Udoma agreed (that's wisdom). Thereupon, the case was adjourned by consent to the 26th of May 1953 for a report as to the terms of settlement, which would then be the judgment of the court as insisted upon by Udoma.

Indeed, because of the recalcitrant attitude of the landowners, openly encouraged by Akpabio, the deed of grant for the college could not be executed up to Jan. 1953 when Akpabio was dismissed and removed from the College as Principal. The College needed a Principal capable of maintaining discipline and raising the standard of education and the moral tone of the college generally. On the recommendation of the National Chief Secretary, acting in his capacity as Manager of the College, the National Executive of the Ibibio State Union appointed Sylvester J. Una as the new Principal of the College on 16th Jan. 1954. And, just before leaving Enugu for the centre to campaign for the office of Prime Minister of Independent Nigeria, what did Zik do?

> Dr. Michael Iheonukara Okpara was obviously handpicked to super-
> sede Mr. Ibanga Udo Akpabio and appointed Premier in succession to
> Dr. Nnamdi Azikiwe because, like the latter, Dr. Okpara belonged to the
> Igbo ethnic group. In contrast, Mr. Akpabio was an Annang man of the
> Ibibio ethnic group, who was made to believe that he was next in com-
> mand to Dr. Nnamdi Azikiwe in the cabinet of the Eastern Region of
> Nigeria. ... Thus, the politics of ethnicity was made to triumph over
> meritocracy and the myth of Dr. Nnamdi Azikiwe being detribalised, a
> political intellectual and a dedicated nationalist was exploded for good
> in the Eastern Region of Nigeria.

Effiong Okon Eyo

Dr. Udoma was succeeded in the office of National President, Ibibio State Union, by "Guess who"; Mr. Effiong Okon Eyo of Uyo Local Government Area, who assumed the office on 1st September 1961. It has been shown, in relation to Zik's civilian *coup d'etat* and the Foster-Sutton enquiry, that E. O. Eyo was previously a political diehard supporter of the N.C.N.C. party as a member of the House of Assembly at Enugu in consequence of which he became closely associated with Azikiwe, leader of the N.C.N.C.. The association between the two men grew somewhat quickly and soon ripened into intimacy by reason of which E. O. Eyo came to be regarded as a close confidant of the party leadership, being also a member of the inner caucus of the party. It was in those circumstances that, in 1953, E. O. Eyo, **for a price**, accepted to and did successfully move a "motion of no confidence in the government of the Eastern Region" of which Prof. Eyo Ita of Calabar Province, a minority man, was head and Leader of Government Business. E. O. Eyo, himself also a minority man from Calabar Province, was then an N.C.N.C. party back-bencher in the Eastern House.

The "motion of no confidence in the Eastern Regional Government" was a most controversial one as to its constitutionality within the context of the provisions of the contemporaneous Nigerian constitution. It was, however, adopted by the N.C.N.C. party hierarchy as a political stratagem. Because of its importance, it ought to have been moved by a well-known front bench party man in the House of Assembly - perhaps someone in the running for the leadership of the N.C.N.C. party - and, in the particular instance, by Dr. Kingsley O. Mbadiwe, already nominated in advance by Azikiwe as successor in office to Prof. Eyo Ita. Instead, again as a matter of tactics, it was moved by E. O. Eyo, in utter defiance of the solemn advice of his fellow N.C.N.C. party members of the Eastern House from Calabar Province. The motion was passed. The result was catastrophic. Professor Eyo Ita and his government were ultimately politically destroyed. Also destroyed was the first ever attempt in the Eastern Region of Nigeria at the political fusion of the various strands and elements constituting the plural societies of the region. Azikiwe, having succeeded in his scheme beyond his wildest dreams, formed a new N.C.N.C. party government in the region (unconstitutional) after an election (also unconstitutional) and later installed himself the Premier of the Eastern Region. As recompense, E. O. Eyo was appointed to several positions in the hierarchy of the N.C.N.C. party and offices in the gift of the government of which, perhaps, the most important in financial terms was the Chairmanship of the Eastern Regional Developmental Corporation (ERDC). E. O. Eyo was then reputed as the one man in the Eastern Nigeria to be receiving, by way of emolument annually, a sum far in excess of the official remuneration of the Premier, Zik. In 1956, things fell apart.

When E. O. Eyo was dismissed from his office as Chairman, ERDC, he, in retaliation, charged Dr. Azikiwe with having abused his high office of Premier of the Eastern Region by the misappropriation of a large sum of money, then specified as £2,000,000, of public funds chan-nelled through the Finance Corporation of the Eastern Region as a conduit pipe into the ACB of which Azikiwe was founder, Proprietor and Governing Director for life. Mr. Eyo was expelled from the N.C.-N.C. party with ignominy. It may be recalled that, at the time when the astounding revelation relating to the misappropriation of such a large sum of money was made, Ojike, Minister of Finance in Azikiwe's cabinet, who was alleged to have been used as a cat's paw in diverting the money into ACB, had already been dismissed from, and deprived of, his cabinet post by the Premier of the Eastern Region on the ground of corruption. Ironically, the dismissal was sequel to Chuba Ikpeazu's Commission of Inquiry into the prevalence of corruption in the body politic and in the public services of the Eastern Region under the premiership of Azikiwe. The dismissal of Ojike, in consequence of such an inquiry which was set up by Zik, was ominous and caused not a little sensation and disquiet and a lot of heart searching. The announcement was received with disbelief as, up till then, Ojike was regarded as a minister in the confidence of the Premier and his likely successor of as leader of the N.C.N.C. party of which he appeared a fanatical activist.

During and immediately after the political crisis of 1953, E. O. Eyo was immersed in the inner caucus of the N.C.N.C. and regarded as a sworn enemy of the Ibibio State Union. As a lynch pin of the N.C.N.C., he was the chief instrument for the destabilisation and fragmentation of the Ibibio nation. In Dec. 1953 during the inaugur-ation of the C.O.R. State Movement at Uyo, E. O. Eyo had openly vowed to tear to pieces and make a bonfire of the Union's Constitution of 1948. He had regarded the Union as guaranteeing the unity of all Ibibio people and therefore an obstacle in the way of the growth and exp-ansion of the N.C.N.C. party in Calabar Province. After the resignation of members of the House of Assembly from Calabar Province pract-ically *en bloc* from the party, the N.C.N.C. party had found the province virtually impenetrable. E. O. Eyo, on commission, was determined to change all that. He therefore set out in his fight against the Union with the aim of destroying it, if possible. For the purpose, and even though himself an Ibibio man, E. O. Eyo engaged himself in the format-ion and organising of an association exclusively for Annang people, as a separate and distinct entity from the Ibibio people. He designated the organisation "Annang Welfare Union", purporting it to be an asso-ciation of Annang people designated to act in opposition always to the Ibibio State Union and meant only for Annang elements in Ikot Ekpene and Abak Districts of Ibibioland. To give fillip to the new organisation, which was intended as a spring board for the N.C.N.C. in Calabar Province, it was announced with fanfare that Eyo had been appointed leader of the N.C.N.C. party in replacement of Eyo Ita.

It was one of the principal duties of E. O. Eyo to spread false political propaganda against the Union and its leadership and to drum it into the ears of the Annang people of Ikot Ekpene and Abak Districts that they were a separate and distinct people from Ibibio people, properly so called, that they were better off sticking to Azikiwe and the party in government, and that if they broke away from the Union, of which all of them were then members, their representatives would be handsomely rewarded by appointment as ministers and members of government boards and corporations and their young people would be awarded government scholarships. Then there was the C.O.R. State Movement of which E. O. Eyo was an inveterate opponent. The movement having been formed under the sponsorship, as it were, of the Union, was to be boycotted by the Annang people of Ikot Ekpene and Abak Districts. Despite all these, as soon as E. O. Eyo was expelled from the N.C.N.C. party, he crawled back on all fours, unabashed, begging to be received back into the fold of the Union. He swore, unsolicited and contrary to the established practice of the Union, to be loyal and bear true allegiance and be faithful to the Union, if admitted, and to support with all his might and intellect the struggle for the creation of the C.O.R. State. The union never believed in oath taking before admission or assumption of office after an election, preferring, according to ancient Ibibio custom, to accept everyone on his honour. E. O. Eyo thereby swallowed back hook, line and sinker all the evil propaganda which had previously been identified as having been spread by him against the Union and the C.O.R. State Movement. He denounced his previous activities and retracted his evil speeches against both, as if in a confessional.

The return of the N.C.N.C. party "storm trooper" and the so-called "encyclopedia of the Standing Orders of the Eastern House of Assembly" at Enugu in the person of E. O. Eyo was not altogether unexpected by the Union. It was inevitable. Indeed, at the outset he was warned that he was playing a dangerous political game to the detriment of his own people by electing, for a consideration, to move the motion of no confidence in Prof. Eyo Ita's government of the Eastern Region, and that in the circumstance, he was entering the path of no return in allying himself, at a price, with leaders of the N.C.N.C. party, who were notoriously adept in the practice of sleight of hand and in the politics of ethnicity. It was obvious from the start that, true to type and character, N.C.N.C. party leadership would soon consider E. O. Eyo disposable material after they would have exhausted his usefulness as an activist. After all, Ibanga Akpabio, the grateful faithful, as an N.C.N.C. party Minister of Education and later of Internal Affairs in Azikiwe's cabinet could be trusted to cover the field of Annang Province, then properly demarcated, even if it meant doing so at the expense of Abak District. As was later discovered, the decision by E. O. Eyo to move the "motion of no confidence in the Eastern Regional government" headed by Prof. Eyo Ita was explicable on some grounds other than pure mercenary motive. The reason, apparently, according to those who were intimate with E. O. Eyo, was that, considering his past record with the Nigeria Police as a convicted person of the heinous crime of trafficking in forged currency, he had hoped to have himself rehabilitated by featuring prominently during the debate on the motion and thereby coming to the limelight as a politician and member of the Eastern House. Having been offered the post of Minister of Public Works on strict terms by Azikiwe, he had accepted, believing it as a sure way to rehabilitation and celebrity. It may therefore be said that, psychologically, E. O. Eyo was concerned also with his future career as a politician.

The Union accepted E. O. Eyo back into the fold but not without hesitation, all things considered. The union accepted the thesis that, as a national institution, it embraced all Ibibio people including their sons and daughters, the living and the dead as well as those yet unborn and to be born and those which may be said to be *en ventre sa mere* in accordance with the concept of Ibibio society. One did not become a member by application. Membership of the union did not entail the payment of entrance fees or even sponsorship by anyone. According to the constitution of the Ibibio State Union, "every Ibibio, wherever resident, and every Ibibio family, village, clan and District shall be member of the Ibibio Union". It is impossible to exercise any option.

To that extent, not having been expelled for stated misbehaviour, E. O. Eyo was a member of the union. It came to him as a great relief to be so told. It was the duty of the Ibibio State Union to be compassionate towards him and to accept his unspoken plea for forgiveness notwithstanding the risk such exercise of clemency might entail. It was, however, agreed that, having been so admitted and in the interest of the security of the Ibibio people, E. O. Eyo must not be kept idle since "Satan often finds mischief for idle hands". He must be saddled with responsibility by being placed in such a position which would bring him face to face with the reality of some of the problems which, as an N.C.N.C. party politician, he had created for the union. On admission, E. O. Eyo at once engaged himself in trying to undo the great harm which he himself had directly inflicted on the union. He also threw himself into the battle of the struggle of the minorities in the Eastern Region of Nigeria for their survival as Nigerian citizens as exemplified in the crusade for the creation of a separate state.

In 1962, the House of Assembly of which E. O. Eyo was an Action Group/U.N.I.P. Alliance member of the opposition representing an Uyo constituency, was dissolved by effluxion of time and due process of law for the first time in the crises ridden history of Eastern Nigeria since the region was established in 1951. A General Election was called. E. O. Eyo was naturally a candidate seeking re-election to the House. It fell upon Dr. M. I, Okpara, as Premier of the Eastern Region and leader of the N.C.N.C. party for the first time, to lead the party campaign for the election throughout the region. In the course of campaigning, Okpara visited Ibesikpo in Uyo, the home town of E. O. Eyo, as he was entitled to do in a democracy. He was said to have been obstructed by a mob organised by E. O. Eyo, apparently in imitation of the notorious N.C.N.C. party electioneering tactics of which he was past master. According to the story, E. O. Eyo was himself armed with a double barrelled shot gun and dressed like a hunter with bare body and only a pair of pants around his waist and commanding the mob to go into battle, forgetful of the fact that he was no longer in the N.C.N.C., the party in government, which is always protected by the Nigeria Police Force.

E. O. Eyo was arrested and charged with attempted murder of M. I. Okpara. He was tried, convicted and sentenced to a long term of imprisonment by William O. Egbuna, Esqr., Chief Magistrate, acting as a Judge of the High Court of the Eastern Region, holden at Uyo. An appeal to the Supreme Court of Nigeria in Lagos was dismissed but the term of imprisonment was mercifully reduced. The National Presidency of the Union by E. O. Eyo thus came to an end abruptly and tragically. He had hardly entered into the office when he virtually walked himself into prison. Although his presidency of the union was undoubtedly short lived, he appeared, in another sense, to have made history in that, according to the chronicles of the Union since its foundation in 1928, he had the shortest tenure of office as President. He had held the office for less than 10 months during which period he did nothing for the Ibibio people. By having himself incarcerated for no just cause, Mr. E. O. Eyo most successfully denied himself the opportunity, gracefully given, of proving his mettle as a leader in his own right.

Immediately after the 1962 General Elections into the Eastern House and the installation of M. I. Okpara, as the Premier of the Region, the so-called coalition federal government began to make preparations for the creation of what was termed the Mid-Western Region of Nigeria by the passing of the Mid-Western Region Act No. 6 of 1962. The move was considered as motivated by spite against the Action Group (A.G.) party, led by Chief Obafemi Awolowo, who was said to have refused to join the coalition government under the leadership of Sir Abubakar Tafawa Balewa. But that was another misinformation promulgated by Zik's group of newspapers. The Mid-West Region was approved precisely because the Western Regional government (Awolowo) did not oppose its creation, whereas the Eastern Nigeria government (Azikiwe) fervently opposed the creation of the C.O.R. state and the Northern Regional government (Ahmadu Bello) opposed the creation of the Middle Belt state. Awolowo openly canvassed for 6 states for Nigeria and so, why would he oppose the creation of one of them in his region? Nigerians, please use your God-given common sense and don't always accept everything you read in the newspaper, especially Zik's, as gospel. Anyway, Balewa, was anxious to have formed a national government of all the political parties, at least of N.P.C., N.C.N.C. and A.G.. Then in 1963, with the passing of the Constitution of the Federation Act No. 20 of 1963 by the House of Representatives, Nigeria was declared the Federal Republic of Nigeria, and Azikiwe, as Governor General of Nigeria, slid smoothly into the office of President of the Federal Republic of Nigeria. With this occurrence, the establishment of Benin Province, including Akoko Edo District in Afenmai Division, and Delta Province, including Warri Division and Warri Urban Township area, as the Mid-Western and the fourth region of Nigeria, became a *fait accompli.* A new dimension was thus created in the political situation. A new concept had emerged in the Nigerian political horizon which raised fresh hopes in the breasts of those determined to see that states were also created in the Northern and the Eastern Regions of Nigeria. It was argued forcefully that, if the Western Region could be broken into two, there was no justification for refusing to split the Northern and the Eastern Regions, the Northern being the largest of the original three regions, the other two constituting almost the same size as the Northern.

The Ibibio State Union and the C.O.R. State Movement renewed their strength and encouraged their supporters to ally themselves with the N.P.C. party so as to bring pressure to bear on the party as the senior partner in the coalition government, the *de facto* government of the Federation of Nigeria. The agitation for the creation of the C.O.R. State in the East received a new impetus and was pursued with vigour. In the meantime, E. O. Eyo, the stormy petrel and a born critic endowed abundantly by nature with the instinct for self-destruction, remained locked up in gaol just when his services were most needed. Although most people wished he had not been so naïve as to have exposed himself to the snares of the N.C.N.C. party, his loss was mourned by none, considering his antecedents. It should be noted that during the absence of E. O. Eyo in prison, the leaders of the union exercised collective leadership. It was a powerful team. Despite E. O. Eyo's incarceration or perhaps because of it, true to character, the Ibibio people who more often than not customarily thrive in adversity, became more united and more active than ever before and the union waxed stronger.

It was at once realised that the arrest, trial and conviction of E. O. Eyo was aimed at the destruction of the Union, and the C.O.R. State Movement. The imprisonment of Mr. Eyo had the effect of rallying the Ibibio people in support of the Union and the C.O.R. State Movement. Most remarkably, while the Union, in the absence of imprisoned Eyo, prospered and flourished, Annang Welfare Union had pined away and disintegrated owing to neglect by the people in exercise of their God-given common sense. Consequently, by the time of the military *coup d'état* in January, 1966, Annang Welfare Union, which Azikiwe had formed through his then disciple, E. O. Eyo, an Ibibio man, to ferrociously antagonise the Union, had ceased to exist, which went to show that it was purely a makeshift and artificial creation by partisan politicians and that it had no solid foundation. Azikiwe lost out again.

Bassey Attah

Mr. Bassey Udo Adiaha Attah, who had studied agriculture in the USA was the first Ibibio Union scholar to return to Nigeria, in 19-43. When issued with a reminder that his fees repayment instalments were past due, he first attacked the figure given in his case. He pointed out that the figure of £560 was the one 'churned out' by the dismissed General Secretary of the Union. He said that he was not prepared to accept any figure unless such figure was supported by receipts issued by him in acknowledgement of having received the amount. He maintained that Mr. Usen had given accounts of two separate sums of money whereas he had only received the sum of £130 from the Ibibio Union in 1942, which he had used in defraying the expenses of his return passage. When Mr. Attah was asked to disclose the total amount he received while a student in the USA, he declined to do so but stated that, whatever the amount was, what he knew for certain was that he had already refunded the sum of £100 since his return to Nigeria. He maintained that it was the National Secretariat's duty to produce receipts for the amount recorded against him. (*cunny-cunny*ENI; a receipt is given by the receiver of the money). Much later, Mr. Attah, as National Chief Secretary (appointed on 5th of September 1958), openly denied having received the sum of £670 shown against his name. He accused the Union of having left him stranded in the USA, despite earlier confirming returning by virtue of the £130 he received (as above). He said he had only agreed and accepted that figure in the spirit of compromise at the time (*cunny-cunny*[ENI]; **he** brought up the £130 matter).

On resumption of a national conference of the Union, on the second day when business was about to be started, the National Chief Secretary, Bassey Attah, could not be found anywhere. He had disappeared at night with all the files and papers belonging to the union. He left no information as to his movement nor did he take permission from the Union's National Executive Committee, nor was he granted any leave of absence. The whole conference was thrown into confusion. It was later discovered that, at the close of the meeting on Saturday night, Attah had left for Port Harcourt (PH) in the Rivers Province, a city some 180 miles away from Eket. What was even more distressing, it was reported that, when leaving for PH, Attah had collected a large quantity of copies of the proven false letter of protest supposedly written by the leaders and traditional rulers of Oniong-Nung Ndem - Awa District Council Area, and had enveloped them for distribution to the people who were not at the conference and living in areas as far apart as from Calabar Township to Ikot Ekpene District. In particular, it was mentioned by the Hon. J. A. Etukube, M.H.A., a delegate from Ikot Ekpene, that even though the matter of the protest had been proven false and settled and the petition withdrawn with an apology by the **real leaders** of the people of Oniong-Nung Ndem - Awa District area, as soon as he arrived, Attah made it a point of duty to serve him and those who arrived with him at the same time with copies of the phoney petition. Some copies of the petition were mailed out by Attah to the delegates who were absent at the conference. On leaving for PH, according to the information, he took with him the trunk box containing the books, files and resolutions passed at the conference and was seen posting a copy of the petition of protest to one B. O. Nya at Ikot Ekpene, a delegate who was absent at the conference. Attah was ensuring he had enough evidence to present to his benefactors so as to collect his promised reward for orchestrating the phoney protest.

Mr. E. O. Eyo, who had deserted his mentor, Nnamdi Azikiwe, to return to his kin, the same people he had antagonised for years on behalf of Azikiwe, obviously recognising signs of betrayal and of the facilitator of such betrayal, which signs he was very familiar with, said that he was sadly disappointed in Attah's behaviour as the National Chief Secretary of the Union and Secretary to the Board of Governors of the Ibibio State College, of which he was chairman. In deploring the manner in which Attah had been performing the duties of his high offices, Mr. Eyo maintained that he found Mr. Attah to have been a drag on the Board of Governors because he could never at any time produce the minutes of the meetings and transactions of the Board on time; he was always late at meetings. You see, in order to be paid, Attah still had to show evidence of having orchestrated the phantom protest against the Union, as instructed, in spite of such protest having been proven to be a hoax by direct denial by the leaders of the people alleged to be protesting! Consequently, on a motion moved by the Hon. Akpan Jack Ekpe, M. H. A., and seconded by Obong Japhet A. Udo of Ikot Ekpene, it was unanimously resolved after a lengthy debate that Mr. Bassey Udo Adiaha Attah be forthwith suspended from his office of the National Chief Secretary, Ibibio State Union, pending a proper investigation and determination of the charges against him.

At the heel of the Willink Commission

On the 26 September, 1957, the Secretary of State for the Colonies, the Rt. Honourable Alan Lennox-Boyd, M.P., on the invitation of the Nigerian Constitutional Conference held that year in London, set up a Commission of Inquiry into the fears of the minorities in Nigeria, which commission was headed by Sir Henry Willink as Chairman. It was part of the duty of the commission to ascertain the facts concerning the existence of fears of minorities on the eve of Nigerian independence and to recommend the means of allaying such fears including, if possible, but as a last resort, the creation of one or more new states in Nigeria prior to independence. E. O. Eyo was known to have played a prominent role in the preparation of the memorandum which was submitted to the commission by the C.O.R. State Movement in support of its stance. Unhappily, the whole exercise of enquiring into minorities' fears by the commission proved a fiasco because of entrenched vested political interests. It was a complete washout. No new state was recommended and none created even though the commission had found a large body of fears entertained by the minorities in existence as against the majority ethnic groups. Sir James W. Robertson, the then Governor-General of Nigeria, proved unyielding and obstinate in his opposition to the creation of new states on the mistaken belief that the NPC party, under the leadership of the late Sardauna of Sokoto, Premier of the Northern Region, was irrevocably committed to the policy of non-admissibility of the proposal to create any new state in Nigeria. Rather, Sir Robertson was harping on the application to Nigeria of the Wales arrangement in Great Britain whereby, in each minority area, a minority council would be set up.

In the circumstances, the leadership of the N.C.N.C. party, on the erroneous assumption that the last word had been spoken on the question of the creation of states, especially in the Eastern Region, proclaimed itself victorious over the minorities. The minorities in the

Eastern Region, who were most vociferous in the crusade for the creation of states, were considered humiliated, worsted and vanquished in the battle for states. And, so it appeared at the time. Azikiwe, leader of the N.C.N.C. and Premier of the Eastern Region, feeling himself on top of the world and conqueror on the occasion like Alexander the Great of ancient Greece, proceeded undaunted in the enterprise of splitting on the ground, territorially, the Ibibio and the Annang elements constituting the Ibibio State Union into two separate peoples, despite a vehement protest by the people of Abak, all in a last ditch effort to split up the Union. For the purpose, he established by legislation the Annang Province and the Ibibio Province, the latter being later changed to Uyo Province, probably as a result of a prick of conscience, being obviously too pointed on the ground of perpetration of an injustice, having named geographical areas with tribal names.

The two separate provinces of Annang and Uyo having been so established, it became clear that the N.C.N.C. party government of the Eastern Region had succeeded in its aim of frustrating the integration of not only the Annang and the Ibibio elements but also the minorities inhabiting Old Calabar Province, in the microcosm and by extension, the Ibibio Union having been the facilitator of the C.O.R. State movement, the minorities of that movement, in the macrocosm. In the new Calabar Province created by legislation, Azikiwe, Premier of the East, also established the Ntoe of the Quas and the Muri of the Efuts to operate as the perpetual rivals of the Obong of Calabar, because the latter was a keen and dedicated supporter of the C.O.R. State Movement. This same Nnamdi Azikiwe, when it was convenient, had declared, through Michael Okpara, that Igbos do not have chiefs, all in the effort to have an upper house instead of a house of chiefs instituted in the East! The establishment of Annang and Uyo Provinces was complete once notices were published in the official government gazette which set out to define the boundaries of the two provinces. Boundaries were then fixed on the ground, with sign boards displayed prominently, regardless of the fact that some Ibibio elements were enclosed within the so-called Annang area and vice versa. Having thus dismembered Old Calabar Province, Azikiwe felt that he had accomplished his self-appointed mission by successfully obstructing the creation of the C.O.R. State, but as often happens, he had left his footprints in the sand!

The Opobo Port Dilemma

Sir Udo Udoma wrote in "The Story of the Ibibio Union:

As a member of the Federal House of Representatives, the highest legislature in Nigeria, which legislature along with the Senate constituted the apex legislature in Nigeria, I moved a motion calling upon the federal government of Nigeria to reopen the sea port at Opobo (now Ikot Abasi), which had previously been closed down for no just cause, by having the bar at the estuary of the Ikot Abasi river dredged so as to enable ocean-going vessels to re-enter into the port for the purpose of unloading or discharging and reloading cargoes for transportation to lands beyond the seas. The motion succeeded and it was unanimously passed by the House of Representatives and accepted, not by the Minister for Transport but, by the Prime Minister himself, the Honourable Alhaji Abubakar Tafawa Balewa of blessed memory. In accepting the motion on behalf of the federal government, the Honourable the Prime Minister spoke in glowing terms in praise of the mover of the motion whom he described as a man of vision. The motion having been accepted by the federal government, as an earnest to the acceptance of the motion aforesaid, **money by way of a token sum was provided for the project in the estimates** indicating that the federal government was intent on prosecuting the project consisting of the dredging of the bar and the construction of a befitting harbour where ships could be moored.

The Opobo port did not belong to Dr. Udoma or his Ibibio people. It was a Nigerian port that had brought Nigeria fame from before the days of King Jaja. Besides, the dredging of the silted bar was an emergency project because of the hardship caused by the congestion at the Apapa port. But any bill moved by Dr. Udoma that had the unavowed support of Government, his adversaries, was not going to see the light of day if Zik could help it! He would rather see the vote for it go to Koko port that no one had canvassed for. Sir Udoma says:

Perhaps, it should be explained that Opobo port (now Ikot Abasi port), from the time of the establishment of the Oil Rivers Protectorate of 1891 by the British government, was an on going, prosperous and a well known port patronised by ocean going vessels for the discharging of commodities and manufactured goods from overseas in exchange for palm oil and palm kernel. For those purposes, there was established by British companies trading in the river a bulk oil plant for the purification and storage of palm oil before shipment in tankers to overseas markets. There was also established a Customs Department under the charge of a senior collector of customs and his staff. As a result of the provision of such facilities, Opobo (now Ikot Abasi) port participated in the trade of the world and became a well known established port in Nigeria, blessed with prosperity. So famous and prosperous was the port all along until, unfortunately, during the period of the second world war (1939-45) when ships departing from the port became easy targets for German U-boats prowling along the Atlantic ocean with the result that some of the ships were attacked and made to sink, the port being naturally open to the Atlantic ocean into which the Ikot Abasi river empties itself. Consequently, in order to avoid sustaining heavy losses due to the activities of German U-boats as enemy, it was decided by the British government that ocean-going vessels should be forbidden from entering into and departing from the port since it was not fortified for security. Thereupon, the port remained closed to ocean-going vessels.

In consequence of the port remaining unused during the period of the war, the bar became silted up so that, at the end of the war, it was considered unsafe for any ocean-going vessel to enter into the port. On proper and thorough examination, it was confirmed that the bar had silted up and that without proper dredging it would be dangerous for ocean-going vessels to be allowed to navigate into the port. Thereupon, the government declared the port closed and the Customs Department and marine officers stationed in the port area were removed and transferred elsewhere in the county, because the cost of dredging the bar and constructing a harbour was considered and placed at a very high figure of the order of twenty one million pounds (£21,000,000) at the time as estimated; that estimate was given by the Development Department in the Nigerian Secretariat in or about 1947. Thus came to an unexpected end the port of Opobo (now Ikot Abasi port), which for many years had served Nigeria well and was considered one of the natural, useful and famous ports in Nigeria with a long history of connection with the British colonial system. Unhappily, by reason of such closure, Nigerians were denied the use of their ancient port even up to 1959 when most of the **active ports in the country were rather congested with ships forming queues in the Lagos harbour for instance,** without a proper berth in the harbour for such ships to be moored - hence my motion in 1959.

Then in November 1959 following upon the dissolution of the House of Representatives, I contested the election with a view to be returned to the House of Representatives of which I had been a member since its inception in 1952. Unfortunately, I failed to be elected **because of heavy rigging induced by the NCNC party [Nnamdi Azikiwe]**, that being the party in government. I was then a member of the UNIP, that is, the United National Independence Party, which was in opposition in the Eastern House as well as the House of Representatives in alliance with the Action Group party. The result of my having failed in the elections of 1959 was disastrous. ... The project was not executed. Rather, the money voted for the project was diverted into the dredging and construction of Koko port in the Mid-Western region of Nigeria perhaps because of the influence of Mr. Festus Okotie-Eboh, [this author says, "No; really, he only carried out what his party leader demanded of him."] then Minister of Finance in the federal cabinet at Lagos. All the same, there was a strong feeling abroad that if I had been returned to the House of Representatives after the election as a member, ... government would have been bound to pursue the project concerning Opobo port according to their pledged word in accepting the motion. Thus, in consequence of my having failed in the election, Opobo port was denied the privilege of being reopened because the federal government under the same Prime Minister had failed in its duty to dredge the bar ... and construct the harbour for the mooring of ocean-going vessels. As it happened, my successor as member of the House of Representatives, because of inexperience, did not follow my lead. My motion, even though it had been passed unanimously in the House of Representatives and accepted by the federal government of the day, had remained a dead letter and Ikot Abasi port has remained still closed even today as I write these lines.[8]

Cunny-cunny master again prevailed in antagonising Dr. Udoma and Ibibioland but depriving Nigeria the use of her famous port.

The *Story of the Ibibio Union, Unabridged*

The *Story of the Ibibio Union* (p. xx) is a book Sir Udo Udoma wrote on the history of the Ibibio Union that sponsored him, along with four others, for university studies abroad, and which book he tagged "An Educated Person's Handbook for National Integration". When he introduced the concept of federalism and states creation into the psyche of Nigerians in 1949, he influenced the Union, he then President, to change its name to *Ibibio State Union* , which act the Ibo Union copied under Jaja Anucha Nwachuku's presidency. He also founded a newspaper, "*Eastern States Express*", at Aba township, to Azikiwe's chagrin. The book also featured Azikiwe's machinations in the Eastern House that led to the removal of Eyo Ita and his constitutionally elected government, after he successfully orchestrated for the House to be dissolved and fresh elections held, even though a sitting member of the Western House of Assembly at the time. He also unconstitutionally sat election for Premier to fraudulently take over the government of the Eastern Region of Nigeria.

So, Azikiwe was not going to sit down and allow the book to be launched. He had to ensure that it did not see the light of day. Goodness knows how he was able to get the publishers of the book to bastardise it. Anything whatsoever that was written about Azikiwe or his cohorts was altered and portions of a chapter of the book would be chopped and wedged in the middle of another chapter, for instance, the idea being that a book so bastardised would not get launched or sold. When he heard that a launching ceremony had been arranged, anyway, the N.C.N.C. incensed disruption of the activities of the Ibibio State Union of the 1950s, also described in the book, had to be made to rear its ugly head in 1987. On his way to the launching of the book in Uyo, Sir Udo Udoma's motorcade was mobbed and prevented from getting to the launch venue. The book was never launched and he never realised any royalty from the books' sale despite having paid a large sum of money to Spectrum Books, Ltd. for it to be published and sold. Apparently, boxes of the adulterated book were given to one of his sons (guess who) and he, accordingly stored them away in a back room of his house without even bothering to read or sell any.

On discovering all of the above, the author has since republished the book from its original manuscript, which book is now available on the *amazon* websites around the world. It makes for very interesting reading. It is the source of much of what is contained in this appendix.

Francis Akanu Ibiam

Re: MacGregor Training College: Francis Akanu Ibiam, who later served as the Governor of the Eastern Region of Nigeria was trained as a medical doctor abroad by the Church of Scotland Mission and returned to eventually head the Mission's hospital in Itu where he was regarded as "the" doctor, by the people. As President of the Ibibio State Union, Dr. Udo Udoma received a report towards the end of September 1949 that representatives of Edere Mbak Ikot Ema had reported to the Union's head office that the Education Authority of the Church of Scotland Mission, of which Mr. Lewars was Secretary, had decided to establish a teachers training college, to be known as the MacGregor Training College, to the memory of the late Revd. Mac-Gregor, a Scottish missionary who, as a pioneer, had spent years of service among the people of Itu. The college was to be built at a site already selected by the Education Authority at Mbak Ikot Ema Village of which Obong Udo Idiong Ekiko was head. On being approached, Obong Ekiko, being an illiterate, along with his people in the village council, in good faith, had sought the advice of Ibiam, as their mission doctor, and Dr. Ibiam strongly advised them against the granting of the land to the Education Authority on the ground that, **if they did, they might run the risk of being ejected from the whole of their village land by white missionaries.** On the strength of Ibiam's advice, Chief Ekiko refused to grant the land required. Unbeknownst to them, Ibiam had then gone and consulted his chiefs in his hometown of Afikpo, exhorting them to, as a matter of urgency, find a suitable piece of land for the Church of Scotland Mission to build them a teachers training college. Very cosmopolitan, right? What treachery!

Anyway, on the strength of the information so supplied by the representatives of the village, the Ibibio State Union decided, in the interest of Ibibio and all Calabar Province people, to intervene, which it did, then oblivious of Ibiam's treachery. For that purpose, a delegation under the leadership of Udoma, the National President, set off on a visit to the people of Mbak Ikot Ema to ascertain the facts. On arrival, the delegation succeeded in prevailing upon Obong Akpan Udo Idiong Ekiko and the whole people of Mbak Ikot Ema to agree to execute the lease of the land required to the Education Authority of the Church of Scotland Mission after Obong Akpan Udo Idiong Ekiko, in exculpation of his conduct in the affair, had placed all the blame for his refusal to have executed the lease of the land, when presented, squarely on the shoulders of Akanu Ibiam, their "trusted" local medical doctor who was in charge of the Church of Scotland Mission Hospital. Without mentioning the traitorous circumstance that provoked Obong Ekiko's refusal, Udoma gave the good news to the Church of Scotland Mission, but then it was too late. The Education Authority, with the prior app-roval of the synod, had decided to site the MacGregor Training College at Afikpo on the site, apparently, already allocated by the people of Afikpo for the purpose, they claimed. My! When did all that happen? The saveface explanation finally given was that it had been decided by the synod of the Church of Scotland Mission, Eastern Provinces of Nigeria, that, in the event Obong Akpan Udo Idiong Ekiko and his people of Mbak Ikot Ema village should refuse to grant the land already selected for the training college, then the institution was to be taken to Afikpo where land **had already been offered** to the Education Authority for the purpose. *Cunny, cunny*! You can tell that to the marines!! If the Afikpo site had already been offered why was it necessary to request land from Obong Ekiko? The things igbos did to "mmong people"! Anyway, the synod's decision to site MacGregor Teachers Training College at Afikpo proved irrevocable. It was peremptory and MacGregor Teachers Training College finally found its home at Afikpo, the home district of Dr. Francis Ibiam.

Re: Ibibio Merchants of Light: Here's another excerpt from "The Story of the Ibibio Union", which speaks for itself:

As if from the blue, there was published in the *Nigerian Sunday Times* issue of 16th April 1961, a statement attributed to His Excellency, the Nigerian Governor of the Eastern Region of Nigeria, Sir Fran-cis Akanu Ibiam, who assumed the office as successor to Sir John Stapl-edon at the Independence of Nigeria. In the statement, the Governor was reported as having called "for the immediate resuscitation of **the Ibibio State Union** which he noted was defunct". The utterance was regarded as an astonishing statement to have come from Her Majesty's Governor of the Eastern Region of Nigeria. The statement was indeed in very bad taste as it expressed a very bad form of mockery, a manifestation of ethnic tendency and jingoism of the worst type. It also indicated a feeling of elation in the misguided belief that Azikiwe, who until then was an active political leader of the N.C.N.C. party to whom Ibiam owed his appointment, had successfully destroyed the Ibibio Union and fragmented the Ibibios by the creation of an Annang Province.

The reaction of the Union was swift. Various District and Branch Unions protested to the National Secretariat. It was necessary to indicate to the Governor the wrath of the Ibibio people as a whole because of such a rash statement on his part. Most Ibibio people who previously held Ibiam in high esteem felt aggrieved that such a statement should have been issued from one who was the holder of the highly respected office of Her Majesty's Governor of the Region, which was considered an office of public trust and confidence and therefore the citadel of the highest and God-given integrity, sobriety and impartiality for which expatriate holders of the office before him were famous. The Governor, if anything, should have been expected to err on the side of affording protection to the weak and the minority, and not to act as a megaphone of a political party or sound an ethnic horn of victory. It, therefore, became the duty of the National Chief Secretary of the Union, the Hon. Anthony George Umoh, on the direction of the National Executive Committee, to address a letter to His Excellency, the Governor. The letter was dated the 29th of April 1961 and read in part:

As well intentioned as your Excellency's fatherly advice was and as much as the Ibibio (people) do appreciate this intention, I am further directed to state most humbly, if emphatically, that the Ibibio State Union has never been defunct and to crave your kind indulgence to ask that your Excellency be graciously disposed, in the interest of the great reputation of the said Ibibio State Union, which is at stake, to either cause the publication to be refuted in your name or that all references to the said Ibibio State Union, as being defunct, be withdrawn.

The letter evoked a reply. On the 3rd of May 1961, one Mr. R.J. Graham, who described himself as Secretary to the Governor, in his scornful letter addressed personally to "Dear Mr. Umoh" thereby avoiding the recognition of the latter as the National Chief Secre-tary of an existing, active Ibibio State Union, wrote:

"His Excellency has asked me to thank you for your letter of 29th April and to say that he is very pleased to learn that the Ibibio State Union is not defunct.

2.   For your information, His Excellency's exact words were:-

' I remember the Ibibio Union that collected money and sent people overseas on scholarships. It is a sad thing that it is now defunct. Please revive it and take a step in training your own sons and daughters etc., etc.'

3.   His Excellency would be very interested to hear details of scholarships etc. awarded by the union over the past few years and we will also arrange for a suitable release to be issued to the Press if you think this to be absolutely necessary."

When the letter was read at the next meeting of the Ibibio State Union National Executive Committee, it evoked a heated debate. It was clear to everyone that the reply disclosed abysmal ignorance and a deep seated ethnic prejudice. Ibiam was a member of the ethnic group in the

Eastern Region of Nigeria which constituted the majority and formed themselves into the political party known as the N.C.N.C.. Thus, Ibiam had manifestly identified himself with the N.C.N.C. party instead of remaining neutral as should have been expected of a Head of State. In the letter, Ibiam failed to disclose the circumstances which had prompted the statement or as to how it came about that the Ibibio State Union, a cultural organisation of the Ibibio people, should have become the subject of a discourse in high Government circles. It was a matter for shame that, whose education was sponsored by missionaries for which, as *quid pro quo*, he had to serve as a mission doctor at Itu in Ibibioland, should have had the effrontery to challenge the Union.

It was rather incomprehensible that, while **the sons and daugh-ters of his ethnic group were being awarded government scholar-ships and being educated overseas at public expense**, Ibiam should have called upon the Ibibio State Union to organise its own scholarship scheme. Such a call only served to reinforce the complaint by the Ibibio people that Ibibio sons and daughters were being discriminated against by the government of the Eastern Region in the award of scholarships. It was considered most insolent for Dr. Ibiam to call for statistics from the Union as to the scholarships awarded by it. It was astonishing that Ibiam did not call for similar statistics from his Ibo State Union.

The real cause of Ibiam's antagonism towards the Union was because the Ibibios had been fighting for a separate state to be created for the minorities in the Eastern Region within the framework of the Federation of Nigeria. And Ibiam, having been appointed by the N.C.-N.C. party government as Governor of the Region, hated the guts mani-fested by the Ibibio people in fighting for all the minorities in the Re-gion. Such a statement made by him would, he believed, endear him to the people of his ethnic group. The National Executive Committee of the Union decided to let sleeping dogs lie and Ibiam was treated as one among those of the major ethnic group to whom the name of the Union was anathema. The statement acted as a stimulus propelling the Union to renew its strength in the struggle for a separate State. ... It did not require an oracle either of Ife or Onitsha, or indeed of Arochuku, if not that the latter had been destroyed by the British expeditionary force in 1902, to discern or prophesy that the country was heading towards disaster. What with the boast of the N.C.N.C. party that it would dominate and rule the country for ever! The Ibibio State Union therefore engaged itself in consolidating its gains and redoubling its efforts prepared for a long struggle, realising that Rome was not built in a day and that nothing ventured nothing gained, "perseverance" being its attribute.

Characters like Ibiam make me wonder how they manage to sleep at night. Albert Einstein once said, "Try not to be a person of success, but rather, try to be a person of value". Is the head of a medical facility who deceives a village chief so that he could take a hospital project promised the chief's people to his own home town a person of value? Is a Governor of a region who, unsolicited and from the blue, as we are told, makes the kind of remark he made about the Ibibio State Union, a man of value? Is he even a happy person? That is obviously something that had been eating at him for a long time! You can sit on as many thrones as you like, but if you are not a person of value, you are nothing! African American activist, Bayard Rustin, said:

> If we desire a society of peace, then we cannot achieve such a society through violence. If we desire a society without discrimination, then we must not discriminate against **anyone** in the process of building this society. If we desire a society that is democratic, then democracy must become a means as well as an end.

The Louis P. Ojukwu Connection

On pages 219-220 of Sir Udo Udoma's book (ref), we find:

> After the inauguration of the Premier of the Eastern Region and the adjournment of the House of Assembly, it was announced with fanfare that Dr. Azikiwe, the Premier, **accompanied only by Mr. L. P. Ojukwu**, a well known business man and transporter as Adviser, was undertaking an Economic Mission to Europe and North America. The Premier didn't take any Minister or Parliamentary Secretary with him, probably on the grounds of frugality. Moreover, there was issued no statement of government policy in relation to the overseas economic mission, nor any programme nor itinerary to be followed by the Premier and his sole Adviser.

> On his return from the overseas mission, the Premier took time to prepare his report, which took the form of a booklet entitled: *A plan for the Rehabilitation of Eastern Nigeria*, the main purport of which was the advocacy of the investment of a substantial sum of money from the accumulated funds of the Eastern Nigeria Marketing Board by the Eastern Regional Government, of which he was Premier, as equity capital in the acquisition of the shares of the African Continental Bank Limited. (Proprietors', directors' and shareholders' names were not disclosed).

The Hidden Clue - Zik's Footprints in the Sand

Like Francis Ibiam, the word "Ibibio" was anathema to Nnamdi Azikiwe and he set out to denigrate anything Ibibio as shown above. He thought that the greatest obstacle to his brainwashing of the Igbo nation in order to have it as accomplice in his efforts to accomplish his dream of being the first Prime Minister of independent Nigeria and the richest man in Africa were Dr. Udo Udoma and his Ibibio State Union. It was not as if they were at war with him. It was simply because the tandem was visionary and progressive enough to have galvanised all the non-igbos in the Eastern Region into a united group, which group constituted a barrier to the achievement of his dream, petroleum oil being in their united geographical area. If the C.O.R.

state movement succeeded, the minorities of the Eastern region would be severed from igbos and their petroleum resources to boot! Since Zik imagined that if his machinations ever hit a brick wall, he would have to resort to the use of the army to break it down, he started early to transform the army into a usable weapon. He discovered right away a main snag; the then longest serving soldier was an Ibibio man, Wellington Bassey! So, when the time would come for the white people to leave, an Ibibio man would head the Nigerian army! Ibibio again!!

Here's what Major General Adeyinka Adebayo said in an interview:[23]

> Q: You were the 7th commissioned officer in 1953, tell us about some of your contemporaries. How did you feel being in the class of the first set of Nigerian army officers?
>
> A: Well, we were 9 officers from Nigeria, drafted into the RWAFF. Fred Ugbomah was NA1, Duke Wellington Bassey, who we nicknamed "Old Bassey" because he was oldest of us after Ugbomah left the Army. His (Bassey's) number was NA2. Aguiyi-Ironsi was NA3, Samuel Ademulegun was NA4, Ralph Sodeinde was NA5, Babafemi Ogundipe was NA6, I wa NA7, Zakari Maimalari was NA8 and Omar Lawal was NA9.

But guess what? The next longest serving was an igbo man, Thomas Aguiyi-Ironsi, who had a record of exemplary duties, and so nobody would raise eyebrows if he was made GOC. Then, there was another small matter to take care of, too. If there was ever a coup attempt and the army took over, Aguiyi-Ironsi would have to appoint military prefects to oversee the regions. So, he had to also ensure that the right army officer would be sent to the East. He would manoeuvre Nwafor Orizu into his office of Senate President when vacating it so that Orizu could ensure that Emeka Ojukwu was doubly promoted to supercede any officer of Eastern origin, including "old man" Wellington Bassey, in readiness for that eventuality, despite Ojukwu having been commissioned only in 1958! A pundit even wrote:

> During the period between 1960 and 1965 **Ironsi, Ademulegun, Ogundipe, Maimalari, Adebayo, Kur Mohammed** and **Shodeinde** all superseded him in rank **for reasons that are not totally clear.**

On the next page we find a list of 30 of the topmost Nigerian officers in Nigeria's military as at **June 1959**, before Azikiwe became the President of the Senate in 1960 and had access to the records. The list was issued from the records of the Army headquarters but is not exhaustive because conspicuously missing are Babafemi Ogundipe and Kur Mohammed. Also, Umar Lawal had passed through transition just before the picture was taken. Anyway, the last statement says:

> The very first Nigerian to be commissioned officer was "Wellington Bassey" with Army number (N1). Two months later "Aguiyi-Ironsi" (N2)

First Generation of Army Officers as at June 1959

HQ Nigerian Army
FROM THE RECORDS: The first 30 Nigerian officers in Nigeria's military.

Date: **June, 1959**

Left to right sitting: Captain Robert Adeyinka Adebayo, **Captain Philip Effiong, Captain Ume Ogere Imo**, Major Samuel Adesoji Ademulegun, **Major Wellington Bassey**, Major General Norman Forster (GOC, Nigerian Army), **Major Aguiyi Ironsi**, Major Ralph Adetunji Shodeinde, Captain Zakaria Maimalari, **Captain Conrad Nwawo**, Captain David Akpode Ejoor.

2nd Row Standing: Lt Igboba, Lt George Remunoiyowun Kurubo, (non Nigerian standing next to Kurubo), Lt J Akahan Akaga, Lt Patrick Awunah, Lt Louis Ogbonnia, **Lt Chukwuemeka Odumegwu Ojukwu**, Lt Eyo Ekpo, Lt Arthor Unegbe, Lt Abogo Largema.

3rd Row Standing: Lt Hillary Mbilitem Njoku, 2nd Lt Macauley Nzefili, 2nd Lt David Ogunewe, 2nd Lt Shadrack, Lt Alexander Madiebo, 2nd Lt Anthony Eze, Lt Yakubu Gowon, 2nd Lt Sylvanus Nwanjei, Lt Yakubu Pam, 2nd Lt Hassan Katsina.

The very first Nigerian to be commissioned officer was "Wellington Bassey" with Army number (N1). Two months later, "Aguiyi Ironsi" (N2) and "Samuel A. Ademulegun" (N3) were also commissioned. A short while later, "Ralph Adetunji Shodeinde" (N4) was also commissioned officer.

(Ref: 22

and "Samuel A. Ademulegun" (N3) were also commissioned. A short while later "Ralph Adetunji Shodeinde (N4) was also commissioned officer.EN6

Notice that all the above named officers, as at June 1959, were each designated as **Major** and that the then GOC, Major General Norman Foster, is flanked in the picture by Majors Wellington Bassey and Aguiyi-Ironsi, being the next two ranked below him. Also, while Philip Effiong, Ume Imo, Conrad Nwawo and David Ejoor were then Captains, both Yakubu Gowon and Odumegwu Ojukwu were Lieutenants. Seeing is believing, isn't it?! What this tells us is that Major Wellington Bassey, who joined the Nigerian Army in 1936 and fought in the 2nd World war in 1944, was in good standing with the colonial officers of our army up till when they had to hurriedly depart in 1964-5, due to machinations by Azikiwe and his crony, Prince Orizu, as David Ejoor has attested to. Further, the above tells us that not only was Bassey wilfully suppressed when military governors were later appointed, so were Philip Effiong and Ume Imo, all because they were either Ibibio or Efik and specifically to elevate Ojukwu, who was only commissioned in 1958, as a 2nd Lt, to the rank he had when Aguiyi-Ironsi appointed military Governors in 1966. First of all, what could Wellington Bassey (N1) have done wrong between the time that picture was taken in 1959 and those appointments were made, to leave him, Bassey, in the doldrums but award him a tribe change for his meritorious three decades service to his country, Igbo nation, please? What did Philip Effiong or Ume Imo, both also higher ranked than Ojukwu, do wrong? Even Igbo nation can clearly see that hell was empty then and all the devils were in the Senate! Be reminded that Nwafor Orizu objected when the ministerial cabinet elected Zanna B. Dipcharima to deputise as Prime Minister during the period Balewa could not be located. The indiscriminate promotion of Ojukwu was no doubt facilitated by Nwafor Orizu out of nothing but Igbo affinity.

Let me tell you non-former Calabar Province people a little something about Ibibios and Efiks. They are siblings by virtue of historically being, along with Annangs and the Oron people, branches of the same tree. However, no Ibibio person would ever make the mistake of filling a form and designating him or herself as Efik. Any Ibibio man's record anywhere that designates him as Efik was surreptitiously altered as assuredly were Wellington Bassey's records in the Nigerian Army after Azikiwe entered the Senate. Everything written about the Nigerian army, after Azikiwe's tenure as President, whether by whites or blacks, have Wellington Bassey as being an **Efik**. He was an **Ibibio** man; I know his family well. His wife knew me, as do his children and grand children. I even hosted her twice in my home in New Jersey and as fate would have it, she and my mother passed on around the same time in 2015 and were admitted to adjacent beds in my friend's medical centre in Ikoyi as their transitions approached. I participated in part in her funeral obsequies. Yes, people may start thinking that Aguiyi-Ironsi may have set about disenfranchising his earlier comm-issioned colleague to take advantage, but the intrigue had occurred before he was in any position to do anything. The malicious act was orchestrated by orders from a higher placed Nigerian after our colonial masters left, whether or not with Ironsi's assistance, though he was one of the beneficiaries of the subversion carried out on military ranks. Igbo nation is always complaining about not being given a chance to rule despite forays by Azikiwe, Aguiyi-Ironsi and Ekwueme. I have never heard any Igbo say, "Come oh, what about *ndi mmong*EN3?"

Is it not ironic that Igbos, who were the greatest critics of states creation and who were the first ones to want to secede, are now the ones who cannot get enough of states? Well, except, really, they did not try to secede by themselves! They wanted to take along the same people they despised and antagonised who, as a consequence, were even desirous of severing ties with them! Every argument that came out of their mouths when it came to the fate of the former Eastern Region or their Biafra was "Igbos are this" or "Igbo's are not that" but whenever they draw the map of their so-called Biafra, up till today, it includes the former Calabar, Ogoja and Rivers provinces - the same people they suppressed and antagonised, and who **are not Igbo, according to Igbos, because they have chiefs and Igbos don't have chiefs!** Yet, Ojukwu sent three separate delegations to Sir Udo Udoma, an *mmong man* who was called the devil by *Henry the Igbo Enter-tainer*, in Uganda in an effort to get him to come and join Zik's fold - the same person Zik wanted to see bankrupt, Ibiam ridiculed and Oj-ukwu ordered his soldiers to pillage his home and school premises in Ikot Abasi township (Alhaji Asare Dokubo even told the author that some of Sir Udo Udoma's books ended up in his own father's house); why? Sir Louis Mbanefo even offered Udoma his position as Chief Ju-stice of Biafra to induce his allegiance! Why? Who told Ojukwu that Mbanefo and Chike Obi were Udoma's friends for him to have them head two of the delegations he sent to lure Udoma to join Zik's fold?

Who was impatient for our colonial masters to go without a gestation period for him and other independence cabinet members to learn the ropes? Who said to their faces that they deserved "the fate which had befallen the Stuart King who was beheaded as a tyrant"? Who dreamt of executive leadership of Nigeria at independence by *"cunny-cunny"*,ENI as David Ejoor testified? Who despised federalism and blamed the McPherson constitution for loosing out in the Western Region? Who detested Ibibios and what they represented to him? Who always carried out his subversive activities remotely, using stooges to carry them out? Who was "giving a lecture at Oxford" when he was supposed to be supporting the Western region's agitation to have Lagos remain in that region, according to the solid agreement he and Awolowo had, leaving Okpara and Mbadiwe to argue **against it**, after AG's end of the bargain on behalf of the NCNC had been fulfilled? Who was ostensibly attending his son's graduation at Lincoln University instead of co-chairing the 1966 Ad Hoc Constitutional conference with Gowon? Who, as President of his country chose the very period of the Commonwealth Prime Ministers' Conference going on in his country to go on a Caribbean cruise for sea breeze, and, oh, just when his tribesmen happened to be staging a military coup to eliminate his political rivals? You know it; newspaper baron, Zik of Africa (in his dreams)!

Cosmopolitan dude, eh?

So, there we have it! Which of Zik's dastardly acts can be deemed to be cosmopolitan or in the mode of "one Nigeria, one country and one constitution"? Is it the general strike of June 1945, which catapulted his name and the NCNC to households in the remotest Nigerian villages and internationally and from which he emerged with enhanced prestige, which strike one of his own former editors, Anthony Enahoro, reported he was believed to have engineered and inspired despite his careful steps to disavow any connections with, as Coleman writes? Is it the civilian *coup d'état* he staged, without jurisdiction, that allowed him to usurp the premiership of the Eastern Region, resulting in the destruction, for good, of the first ever attempt at the political fusion of the various strands and elements constituting the plural societies of the Region? Is it the diversion of funds from the coffers of the ERDC into his private bank he orchestrated while in that office or his partisan pro-Igbo administration that marginalised the minorities in the region and resulted in Southern Cameroun breaking away and the COR state movement forming? Is it the damage to the Western Region and to Nigeria that the machinations of the N.C.N.C. party under him, capped by his 13 Emergency Regulation Acts, brought about? Is it his autocracy - incessant disrespect of the constitution and authority figures but ironic flaunting of authority over subordinates? Or, is it his constant breach of oath and promises like "the solid AG/NCNC Alliance" Chief Benson said he betrayed (pp. 183-6)? Is it the campaign launched to have a Higher House (i.e., Senate) created instead of a House of Chiefs in the East, Michael Okpara lying (Zik conveniently absent) that the

Region did not have Chiefs, thus denigrating the stools of the Obong of Calabar, the Aro of Arochukwu, the Obis of Oguta and Onitsha, and the Amanyanabos that abounded in Riversland? When later, Premier Azikiwe established the Ntoe of the Quas and the Muri of the Efuts to operate as the perpetual rivals of the Obong of Calabar, because the latter was a keen and dedicated supporter of the C.O.R. State Movement, was he not shooting himself in the foot? When the Oputa panel heaped the blame for Nigeria's decadence on army rule, a result of the likes of those machinations, did it not somehow beg the question?

Why am I writing these books? I am 73 years old now, and if any good comes out of these books, I may not be around to see it. But, I know that it is not by mistake that God decided when writing His computer programme for His world, to include code to have me incarnate in the family of my visionary father so see what Yoruba and Igbo people were doing to someone who had dedicated his life to truth and justice, as well as national service. I saw things and I heard things intended for the enquiring minds of humanity. I saw the leaders who were not ambitious, unlike the others, use the small advantage they had, being numbers, to try to move Nigeria forward by having an all representative government, in spite of having won the elections resoundingly, and to set out to stamp out corruption, starting with sensitising the judiciary, and who, in fact, desperately had to send three of their bright students, M. Bello, M. Nasir and Buba Addo, to the UK to study law, and invite Dr. Udo Udoma to come and be the Attorney-General of the North, because there was a dearth of qualified lawyers there, which is why, like visionaries, they needed Nigeria to give herself time to prepare the ground properly for independence before ushering it in, but Azikiwe and Awolowo would hear nothing of it, are the very people that Igbos and Yorubas were blaming for all Nigeria's misfortunes. They did not invite Okotie-Eboh into the cabinet; Azikiwe did! Igbos could not see that, like New Zealand's young Prime Minister, Jacinda Arden, wisely said, "It takes courage and strength to be empathetic". Ahmadu Bello and Abubakar were nothing like, say, Gowon, Abacha or Babangida, military co-facilitators of those misfortunes and who were no different than Nzeogu and Ifeajuna (Ifeajuna being the tribalist responsible for injecting Igbo partisanship into their "revolution" plan), all being military misfits. While the latter were idealistic young men blinded by the hoodwinking of Nnamdi Azikiwe and his cronies, as with "carpet crossing", for instance, and who, inadvertently, propelled Nigeria on a path of no return, in the belief that they were doing us a favour, the former magnified the harm so done by fanning the flame, instead of extinguishing it, ambitious Yakubu Gowon trying to be as

Lieutenant Colonel Gamal Abdel Nasser, the military officer turned politician who served as Egypt's Prime Minister from 1954 to 1970!

You see, as Milan Kundera wisely said: "*We go through the present blindfolded. Only later, when the blindfold is removed and we examine the past, do we realise what we've been through and understand what it means.*" Further, like Justice Oputa wrote: "We have to remember in order to forget, to learn lessons and to forge ahead. Thus, we must know our *terminus a quo* in order to arrive at our *terminus ad quem.*" [if *vested interests* allow us to remove our blindfolds to finally see that blind ambition is the worst enemy of progress.] Remove your blindfolds, Nigerians, and especially, Igbo nation; my books will help you. Horace Mann said, "*Be afraid to die until you have won a victory for humanity*", and knowledge being an acquisition, these resolution books are written in that vane. After all, life is either a daring adventure or nothing, as prolific blind and deaf writer and lecturer Helen Keller intimates. Read them, even if you have to do it in the toilet in the middle of the night so that nobody knows, and think about what you have read. You will see in the O.J. book that *ndi ocha*[EN4] can also be brainwashed, like you were by Zik, into believing what they read or hear in the media. Did Albert Einstein not say that *unthinking respect for authority is the greatest enemy of truth*? Also, start availing yourself of constitution consciousness if you are going to open your mouth to criticise; otherwise, shut your trap! Aba Ngwa was one of Nigeria's melting pots, where the real Cosmopolitans lived, before Zik's and his cronies' hate and inordinate ambition turned Nigeria into something now unrecognisable. This author is an Aba boy, through and through, and loves you all with all his heart. Be well.

ENDNOTES (ENs): EN1 - "*Cunny-cunny*" is a word the author has not heard or seen written in decades but was brought to his attention by a David Ejoor interview. It is one of the words in the Nigerian Pidgin English lexicon of his formative years which means a slew of ulterior motivated actions likened to "sleight of hand", "hoodwink", "dissimulation", "subterfuge", "bluff", "trickery"; etc. In the same lexicon was "i.-t.k." read "I too know" but literally "you think you are smart, eh?".

EN2 - "*mmong*" used to be the Igbos' appellation for Ibibios and Efiks.

EN3 - Thus, "*Ndi mmong*" would translate to Ibibio and Efik people.

EN4 - "*Ndi ocha*" translates to Caucasians

EN5 - "*Bad Man Kalabar*" was Aba Ngwa's favourite cartoon character; exclusive to *Eastern States Express* newspaper!

EN6 - Ugboma, NA1, had left the army when the N system was adopted.

Meet the author!

*"As a student, I never cared to pass the
theory and risk passing the practical."*.

~ Anonymous

Ayanti Udo Udoma was born at Ikot Ekpene, in now Akwa Ibom State of Nigeria, on February 18, 1950. He is the first son of the late world renowned statesman and legal luminary, Sir Udo Udoma, and the late Lady Grace Udoma. He started school at the age of 5 and attended the St. Mary's Convent School, Aba, better known as Sancta Maria, for three years before moving to St. George's School, Aba from where he passed the common entrance examinations to both King's College, Lagos and Government College, Umuahia at 11 years old. Since the interviews were mischievously scheduled for the same day, he only attended that at King's College (KC), passed it and started an active and exemplary all-round scholarship there the following January.

At King's, he represented Harman's House in almost all inter-house competitions and was the scribe for the Harman's House "magazine". He wore the KC colours, at one time or another, in badminton, lawn tennis, field hockey, and cricket, captaining the tennis and cricket first teams before leaving. He represented the Lagos Territory academicals in cricket from 1966 to 1969. In Higher School, he won the Owoaje Cup Competition in Men's Doubles Tennis each year, playing with non-KC partners - his innovation in the spirit of sportsmanship, and he skippered the Lagos Schools cricket team that set all kinds of records at the Morocco Clark Inter-state Cricket competition at the Liberty Stadium in Ibadan in 1969, in addition to winning it all. While at King's, he was President of each of the Science and the Photographic Societies and participated actively in the Dramatic Society, famously featuring in "The School for Scandal".

His sports laurels continued after King's as he went on to play first class cricket for Lagos State, Nigeria and West Africa, along the

126

way leading the University of Lagos cricket team to capturing the gold medal at the West African University Games in Kumasi, Ghana, after annihilating the Fourah Bay College and the University of Ife teams, who were both favoured. A student of the Alan Knot "school" of disciplined wicketkeeping, he is credited as the pioneer of aggressive wicketkeeping in Africa. He was, in absentia, the second selection for the first ever West African cricket team at the trials in Freetown, Sierra Leone in 1975 and stumped England's John Barclay around the leg side off opening bowling in the Lagos, Nigeria test against the then touring Marylebourne CC team that was captained by Colin Cowdry.

An Ivy-league student, Mr. Udoma has two Bachelor's and two Master's degrees - one in each of the S.T.E.M. (Science, Technology, Engineering & Mathematics) disciplines. He has immense experience in cellular phone development as well as both software and hardware quality assurance and design, having worked for many years in the Advanced Communications Technology department of the Bell Laboratories in New Jersey, USA, first as part of AT&T and, after its divestiture, as Lucent Technologies, Inc. He has developed a knack for Research, Data Mining & Knowledge Discovery, computer-aided design and optimization. He is also a volunteer Mathematics instructor.

Mr. Ayanti Udoma also has the purview for publishing and is the in-house publisher of all his father's books, including his Lordship's autobiography, "The Eagle in its Flight", which Ayanti completed after his father's death by adding the last two chapters. Having had the opportunity of having audience with Nigerian patriots like Chief Obafemi Awolowo, Chief T. O. S. Benson, Alhaji Maitama Sule and, of course, Sir Udo Udoma, and to look through his father's rich literary archives in the process of publishing his Lordship's books, he developed interest in the solution of Nigeria's constitutional and social problems and decided to also put "pen to paper", an itch that grew into a preoccupation. He proffered a postulation as to how Nigeria's illegitimate 1999 Constitution might be successfully abrogated by Judicial Fiat, believing as he does that most of the ills of the Nigerian polity which the Muhammadu Buhari administration has highlighted as its immediate targets for cure, are but symptoms of the real problem - the 1999 Nigerian Constitution. That postulation is part of the subject matter of his second book, "The Go-Stop-Go Nigerian Republic - Volume II".

Patrick D. Okonmah wrote that "Written constitutions (any constitution for that matter) represent the collective will of the people expressed as the supreme rules to which all citizens are subject and habitually obey. ... The sacredness of a constitution is born out of the elaborate process through which it is born. It entails the election of representatives to a constituent assembly at which representations from all segments of the Nigerian society are collated and considered." A constitution that is forced on the people by usurpers based on a pack of lies, cannot be said to reflect the collective will of the people or be expected to command their respect. **The preamble of the 1999 Constitution remains blatantly false.** Learned ones, like Professor Ogowewo of the University of London, declared that the 1999 Nigerian Constitution is null and void. It must be abrogated. Now, there are no checks and balances left in the system to instill discipline in the polity, all the way from motorists on the street to the President at Aso Rock. The separation of powers amongst the three tiers of government has proven inadequate in Nigeria to ensure the integrity of the "democratic" process. As intimated before, there is a clear propensity for collusion, which has negated the intended function of power separation and abetted the "coming ashore to breed" of our albatross, politically correctly termed "vested interests - military and otherwise".

Mr. Udoma had earlier accepted the challenge thrown by a Senior Advocate of Nigeria to take a crack at this exposé that debunks the so-called "carpet crossing" theory that characterised the Western Nigeria Elections of 1951-52. Because the five Nigerian giant media houses that were sent copies would not publish the serialised exposé or interview the writer, the article was turned into this keepsake. In exposing the six-decade-and-a-half old propaganda, he has found himself in the unique position of uniting the subjective sympathy of an Eastern Region of Nigeria born-and-bred with the more objective outlook of the patriotic Nigerian familiar with the problems that confront both sides of the issue. Hopefully, all those Nigerians that developed bias against subjects of another tribe based on what now turns out to be mere propaganda can have a rethink and hence a change of heart for the betterment of that dear nation. The "Cold File" investigation of the O.J. Simpson saga was inexorably to follow, the results of which constitute the subject matter of the book *O.J. Simpson Did Not Do It - Guess Who Did*. These writings, along with their being published and promulgated as keepsakes for posterity, have allowed him to unite his divine gifts with his passion for the truth and for justice in the service of his fatherland, Nigeria, and his domicile country, the U.S. of A., his persecution by evil ones notwithstanding.

Mr. Udoma, in posthumous commendation to the visionary statesman and Nigerian political pioneer that was his father, not only credits him with providing both the impetus and the material to tackle many of these tasks, but also thanks him immensely for the literary and stewardship legacy he has left to Nigerians and indeed to posterity. He is steadfastly getting the treasury of knowledge His Lordship left behind to its intended repository - the enquiring minds of humans. All the author's life's contributions are in the spirit of the mission handed down through the generations by his ancestors who now all watch over him, starting with Abasi Akpan Enin, the lead founding father of Ikot Abasi in Akwa Ibom State of Nigeria, including his great, great grandfather, Ayanti Umo Idonho, whose name he proudly bears and after whom the family compound is named and, of course, his loving dad, the Hon. Sir Udo Udoma. He respectfully dedicates his trilogy of resolution books to these three ancestors. He affectionately gives props to Barrister Uko Essien Udom who instigated this "carpet crossing" exposé, Dr. Anthony Osa-Oboh who suggested changing its title and Dr. Yemi Ogunbiyi who lent to the idea of making it a keepsake. He seizes this opportunity to again implore everyone to become constitution conscious so as to adequately contribute to nation building.

While Mr. Udoma is known to be passionate about spirituality and being his "brother's keeper" - facilitating many a life-saving fund-drive or drug rehabilitation, participating in mentoring and evangelism programs, and sponsoring formal and pastoral education and sports competitions, he is also known to play things down, seeing it all as simply the cross he has to bear. The preachment that "if you live the life of God you do the word of God" is to him elementary.

If the readers of his books find the material subjective enough to make interesting reading and objective enough to be intelligent, the author would have succeeded in his endeavour to inform and inspire, while sharing the truth legacy in his custody with his fellow man for the betterment of all, believing as he does in Ma'at - truth and justice, - a philosophy which he shares with many human rights activists.

Malcolm X, who is said to be one of the greatest and most influential African Americans in history and credited with raising the self-esteem of black Americans and reconnecting them with their African heritage, despite being assassinated at the tender age of 39, said:

"I'm for truth, no matter who tells it. I'm for justice, no matter who it is for or against. I'm a human being, first and foremost, and as such I'm for whoever and whatever benefits humanity as a whole.".

Referenced Books / Lecture / Papers

No finite point has meaning without an infinite reference point. ~
Jean-Paul Sartre (French Philosopher)

1. "History and the Law of the Constitution of Nigeria – Unabridged Edition" by the Hon. Sir Udo Udoma

2. "The Story of the Ibibio Union – Unabridged Edition" by the Hon. Sir Udo Udoma

3. "Nigeria: Background to Nationalism" by Prof. James Smoot Coleman

4. "The Eagle in its Flight – Being the Memoir of the Hon. Sir Udo Udoma, CFR".

5. "Organisation and Developments of the Legal Profession in Africa" - by Dr. T. O. Elias

6. "My Odyssey – An Autobiography", (2001 reprint), by Nnamdi Azikiwe

7. "Constitutional developments in Nigeria: An analytical study of Nigeria's Constitution making developments and the historical and political factors that affected constitutional change" by Kalu Ezera

8. "Nigerian Political Parties: Power in an Emergent African Nation" by Prof. Richard L. Sklar

9. "Benin and the Midwest Referendum of 1963" - Lecture by Nowa-magbe A. Omoigui

10. "Musings from the Shelter of the Elephant Rock" by Sir Udo Udoma

11. http://hansard.millbanksystems.com/commons/1956/jul/24/eastern-region-nigeria-commission-of

12. "History of Nigerian Constitutional Development" by Olanrewaju Olamide, posted in NIGERIAN CONSTITUTIONAL LAW

13.   "Corruption in Nigeria: A Historical Perspective (1947 - 1962), part I of 2" by Rina Okonkwo

14.   "Building a Nation - An Autobiography by Chief Dennis Chukude Osadebay"

15.   "The Go-Stop-Go Nigerian Republic" by Ayanti Udo Udoma

16.   http://credo.library.umass.edu/view/pageturn/mums312-b114-i429/ #page/1/mode/1up

17.   "Nationalism and Development in Africa: Selected Essays" by Professor James Smoot Coleman

18.   "Cameroon Political Story: Memories of an Authentic Eye Witness" by Nerius Namaso Mbile

19.   "The Price Of Liberty: Personality and Politics in Colonial Nigeria" by Kenneth W. J. Post and George D. Jenkins

20.   http://www.blackpast.org/gah/nigerian-youth-movement-1934-1951

21.   "Who's Who in the Western House of Assembly", by Public Relations Department, Lagos (1952) [Courtesy of Library of Congress, Washington, DC, USA. See cover below.]

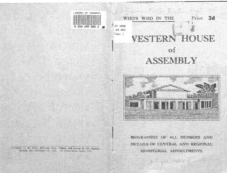

The cover of "Who's Who in the Western House of Assembly"
- copy at the Library of Congress

22.   "https://m.facebook.com/NigerianArmy/photos/a.354471614665170/ 1184601698318820/2type=3

23   Gen Adeyinka Adebayo's last interview: sunnewsonline.com 12/03/17

24.   "The origins of Nigeria's Notorious 419 Scams" by Stepen Ellis on Newsweek.com edition of 05/09/2016 at 10.38 am EDT

Index

I

1951 Constitution   xiii, 4-6, 35, 68
1951 elections   1-6, 8, 10, 15-16, 29, 39, 69, 75, 80-81, 100, 143
1954 Constitution   61
1953 elections   99
1964 elections   50

A

A Reply to Zik – By Chief Arthur Prest   17
A Tale of Two Parties   33. *Also, see* The Tale of Two Parties
Aboderin, Moyosore   11, 15, 20, 24, 51
abrupt adjournment of the House   43-44
Abyssinia   88
Achebe, Chinua   88
Action Group conference at Owo   16
Ad Hoc Constitutional Conference (12/9 - 3/10/66)   xxii, 43-44, 135-136
Adamawa   41
Addison   83
Adebayo, Robert Adeyinka   132-133
Adebola, Haruna P.   11, 24-25, 51
Adedamola, A.   11, 24, 51
Adedoyin, Prince Adeleke   xx, 7, 9, 11, 22, 24-27, 29, 49, 51, 73, 99-100
Adedoyin, William   35
Adegbenro, D. S.   11-12, 19-20, 24, 48-49, 51
Adejare, I. A.   11, 51
Adelabu, Adegoke   11, 14-15, 20, 32, 51
Ademola, Adenekan   80

Ademola, Justice Adetokunbo   48
Ademola II, Alake Oladapo   35-36
Ademulegun, Samuel Adesoji   132-133
Adeoba, S. A.   11-12, 23, 26, 51
Aderemi, Alhaji Adesoji   36-37, 42-43, 47, 54
Adeyefa, S. A.   11, 51
Adigun, J. O.   11, 52
Administrator, the 46, 50. *See* Majekodunmi, Dr. Moses A.
Advanced Communications Technology department   96
African Continental Bank (ACB) xxi, 12, 59, 63-64, 67, 96, 98, 101, 104-107, 113
African mandate system   86
AG ministers   44
AG-NCNC Alliance   xxii, 50, 140
Agbu, P. C.   79-80
Agidee, M. F.   11, 24, 51
Agodi Gardens in Ibadan   10, 26
Aguiyi-Ironsi, Johnson Thomas Imanakwe   xxii, 131-134
Ahmed, A. T.   11, 51
Ajayi, J. Ade   11, 51
Ajeromi-Ajegunle Constituency   49
Akaga, J. Akagan   133
Akarigbo of Ijebu Remo   35
Akeredolu-Ale, O.   11, 24, 51
Akerele, Abiodun   11, 51
Akilu, Brig. Gen. Halilu   58
Akinbiyi, D. T.   11, 15, 20, 24, 51
Akinjide, Richard A.   80
Akinloye, A. M. A.   11, 14-15, 20, 51, 54
Akinola, S.   11-12, 15, 23, 24, 29, 51
Akinsanya, Samuel   70
Akintola, Chief Samuel Ladoke   11, 24, 27, 38, 42-43, 48-51, 54, 78-80
Akinyemi, Samuel A.   11, 15, 20, 52
Ako, J. G.   11, 15, 23-24, 29, 32, 52
Akpabio, Ibanga   xxvi
Akran, Cladius Dosa   11, 52, 54
Akwa Ibom State of Nigeria   vi-vii,

B

C

Other Books by Amazing Grace Publishers

*"The worth of a book is to be measured by
what you can carry away from it.".*

~ James Bryce

BOOKS BY THE AUTHOR'S FATHER

The Eagle in its Flight - Being the Memoir of the Hon. Sir Udo Udoma, CFR was published in 2008 under the name "Grace & Son" and launched in January 2009 while two previous books written by Sir Udo Udoma, *The Story of the Ibibio Union* and *History and the Law of the Constitution of Nigeria,* have since been republished under the present name. A fourth book, *Musings from the Shelter of the Elephant Rock by Sir Udo Udoma, CFR* has also been compiled by this author and published by Amazing Grace Publishers.

A TRILOGY OF RESOLUTION BOOKS DEDICATED TO THREE OF THE AUTHOR'S ANCESTORS

The Go-Stop-Go Nigerian Republic - Volume II and *O.J. Simpson Did Not Do It - Guess Who Did*, both written by Ayanti Udo Udoma, will be released in 2018 by Amazing Grace Publishers along with this one - the trilogy of resolution books being dedicated to his late ancestors: **Abasi Akpan Enin**, the lead founding father of Ikot Abasi village, township and local government area, **Ayanti Umo Idonho**, after whom the family compound is named and whose name he proudly bears, and **Sir Udo Udoma**, his father and authoring mentor.

Here's the line-up of the books [other than this one] published by Ayanti's publishing companies:

OTHER UDO UDOMA BOOKS

❋   ❋   ❋

A NOTE ON THE TYPE

Le Monde Livre Classic is a Renaissance style typeface that works beauti-fully on text and titling settings. Designed by Jean Francois Porchez as an extension of Le Monde Livre, this family distinguishes itself by its historical forms and by its stylistic effects. **Le Monde Livre Classic**'s italics follow the models of the Renaissance and feature italic capital and lowercase swashes. **Le Monde Livre Classic** works beautifully for book typography, magazine settings from text to display, while this family, fully rebuilt from scratch in 2012, brings more exuberance in designs.

THE STORY OF THE IBIBIO UNION
By Sir Udo Udoma
ISBN: 978-1-7342415-2-5

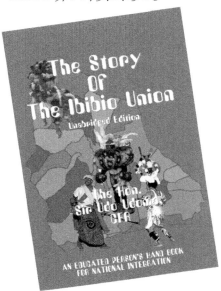

This book lays down the history of the Ibibio (State) Union, as written by an active participant. It is the story of how it all began; an analysis of its imaginative beginning, its inspiring formation, its steady growth and wonderful expansion, its versatility and progress as a national institution, its dynamic flexibility, its arrested evolutionary development in the process of growth, and its untimely proscription as an active, virile and prolific association of a forward-looking, God-fearing, creative, dedicated and self-sacrificing Nigerian minority group in the old Eastern Region of Nigeria.

The author, Sir Udo Udoma, hoped that present and future generations would be able to produce a better history of the Ibibio Union, which has become a landmark in the history of the growth and development of the Nigerian nation. The book was first published by Spectrum Books Limited in 1987. An unsuccessful attempt to release an unabridged edition in hardcopy was made by Grace and Son in 2011, while the release of its paperback version by Amazing Grace Publishers is imminent.

HISTORY AND THE LAW OF THE CONSTITUTION
OF NIGERIA
By Sir Udo Udoma, CFR
ISBN: 978-1-7342415-3-2

In writing this book, the author realised an ambition, which he had developed when he was a Reid's Professor's Prizeman of the Law School of the University of Dublin, Trinity College, Dublin, Ireland, to one day write a book on Constitutional Law. As an undergraduate student of Law, he manifested sound knowledge and keen interest in the study of Constitutional Law and History, Criminal Law, and the Law of Evidence and studied the Constitution of Eire, 1937 and later compared and contrasted the English Constitution and the constitutions of the Swiss Cantons and of the United States of America.

Back to Nigeria, he attended every constitutional conference ever held for the formulation of constitutions for the governance of Nigeria before independence, presided over the Constitutional Court of Uganda when he was the Chief Justice of Uganda in the 1960s, and, in 1977, chaired the Constituent Assembly that prescribed Nigeria's 1978 Constitution. And so, it was befitting and pertinent for him to have written an authoritative source of reference for students of Law as well as legal practitioners in Nigeria and elsewhere. The book was first published by Malthouse Press Limited in 1994. An unsuccessful attempt to release an unabridged edition in hardcopy was made by Grace and Son in 2011, while the release of its paperback version by Amazing Grace Publishers is imminent.

THE EAGLE IN ITS FLIGHT
Being the Memoir of the Hon. Sir Udo Udoma, CFR
ISBN: 978-1-7342415-4-9

   Twenty-seven of the twenty-nine chapters of his autobiography, as well as the appendices, were written by the late Sir Udo Udoma, and are reproduced in his own words. Several years elapsed between the time he put the last dot on this book's manuscript and the time he was called up to glory by his maker. His eldest son, Ayanti Udo Udoma, tried to fill in those years, more poignantly in his own words, by narrating in the remaining two chapters his interaction with his father during that time.

   The book takes the reader through a flight that began at a time of cultural festivities, delving into his ancestral lineage and the British administrative setup of the old Calabar province of the author's youth. The flight continued with his education and his affiliation with Methodism, including his sponsorship by the Ibibio Union to study Law in the United Kingdom where he, not only excelled academica-lly, but sounded a note of warning to the British colonial administration that her wards were coming of age. The flight then had him soaring strongly, with keen vision, through a sterling law practice, political and civil rights struggles, entrepreneurial and mentoring projects, and national service.

   The Eagle In Its Flight is the success story of an African statesman - an accomplished professional, a personality of exemplary character, a mentor to many an aspiring lawyer, judge, rights advocate and industrialist, and a national property of inestimable value. It was first published by Grace & Son in 2008 in hardcopy. The paperback version is expected to be released at the end of 2019.

MUSINGS FROM THE SHELTER OF
THE ELEPHANT ROCK
By the Hon. Sir Udo Udoma, CFR
ISBN: 978-1-7342415-5-6

This book is a mosaic of excerpts from the different writings of the Hon. Sir Udo Udoma that relate to his heritage - the Ibibio people (including the Annang, the Obolo, the Oron and the Efik speaking people) and, in particular, the inhabitants of the village, township, river and local government area that bear the name of his ancestor, Abasi Akpan Enin, the lead founding father of Ikot Abasi in Akwa Ibom State of Nigeria, as compiled by the publisher.

The treasury of knowledge Sir Udo Udoma left to posterity is part of a mission that has been handed down by Abasi Akpan Enin through his lineage, which include's Sir Udo's great grand-father, Ayanti Umo Idonho, after whom the family compound is named.

In this book, Sir Udo also extrapolates on the circumstances and events that necessitated and informed the agitation of minorities for states creation in Nigeria, as well as how the people of Ikot Abasi had to bear the foreign and unmeaning name of "Opobo" for so long in spite of the people's continuous agitation for a name change back to an indigenous one. An enlightening profile of that enigmatic character known as King Jaja of Opobo is included.

THE GO-STOP-GO NIGERIAN REPUBLIC
VOLUME II
By Ayanti Udo Udoma
ISBN: 978-0-9819192-9-4

This book contains a compilation of the synopses of the historical and constitutional events that transpired in the Nigerian polity since the making of the second republic, as seen through the eyes of some constitutional students, political scientists and the press. These events run from the end of Olusegun Obasanjo's tenure as military head-of-state to Muhammadu Buhari's ascension to the executive presidency of Nigeria in May 2015.

Ayanti Udo Udoma republished Sir Udo Udoma's book, **History and the Law of the Constitution of Nigeria**, which covered the Nigerian constitutions from 1914 to the end of the Third Republic. In the process, he decided to pick up the gauntlet from where his Lordship had suspended work and highlight, in two *Afterword* chapters, the events that occurred since then, as a service to the readers of his dad's book. Insight gained by the exercise led him to the postulation, in that chapter's conclusion section, of a novel theory (a blueprint, if you will) of why and how the 1999 Nigerian Constitution might be successfully abrogated by judicial fiat, having concluded that the only way to ensure the stability that Nigerians desired was for the Nigerian people to have representatives of their own enact a constitution that they all could claim ownership of for the first time in Nigeria's constitutional life.

The *Afterword* mentioned above, which covered the period from 1978 up to Goodluck Jonathan's ascension to the presidency in 2011, has now been transferred into this book with the period extended to May 2015. The "Go-Stop-Go routine of Nigeria's civilian governments in exchange with military regimes" is an expression used by Sir Udo Udoma to describe her polity since Independence.

O.J. SIMPSON DID NOT DO IT - GUESS WHO DID

By Ayanti Udo Udoma
ISBN: 978-0-9819192-8-7

This book is the report of the "cold file" investigation conducted by the author to prove that O.J. Simpson could not have committed the murders of his ex-wife, Nicole Brown-Simpson, and her friend, Ronald Goldman. There was a marked dichotomy between the author's take on each of the attendant episodes of the saga against that of virtually the rest of the world that was outraged by the jury's verdict in the criminal case and he wondered why.

If the learned Prof. Gerald F. Uelmen had explained away this dichotomy as "We all wear tinted lenses, but we don't all wear blinders.[14]", and if O.J. Simpson's "God forbid" lawyer, the insightful Prof. Alan M. Dershowitz, had shown how the prosecution's "mountain of evidence", which, along with the damning information it leaked to the press, hoodwinked the world into their state of mind, was at best "mountain range, with a few high peaks, seve-ral smaller hills and a large number of valleys"[12], why was the world, even 22 years after the fact, still outraged? If Double Helix Medal recipients, Barry Scheck and Peter Neufeld, had told America that Simpson, a civil defendant, was prosecuted with more investigat-ive, prosecutorial and reporting resources than did the World Trade Centre bomber, that several fingerprints found at the crime scene, and the DNA associated with blood type B found under Nicole's fingernails, were inconsistent with any known persons, especially O.J. Simpson, and that, yet, no further effort to identify their sources was made, why was nobody asking questions? Does the world know that up till today, the reddish brown spot detectives "discovered" on the door of O.J.'s Bronco, which reason they gave for one of them scaling the wall to allow the others into O.J's mansion to ostensibly "save O.J.'s life" and which they later gave to a judge as reason to obtain a search warrant for the estate, was determined not even to be human blood?

If forensic scientist and detective, Dr. Henry Lee, had said "We don't have EDTA in our body; something wrong!" and if famed attorney Johnnie Cochran described detectives as "Fuhrman, the man who planted the glove and Vannatter, the man who carried the blood", why hadn't the world taken a step back to re-evaluate its thoughts and tried, for the first time, to actually come up with a postulation as to how O.J. managed to do it, in the light of all the unassailable facts we had at our disposal, to date then? For instance, how did Simpson manage to transform from a raging maniacal killer covered in gore, berries and dirt to an affable, bathed and well trimmed celebrity wearing well pressed clothes and an amiable persona, in just 5 to 6 minutes as testified to by driver Allan Park? Why was everyone speculating as to how high the "mountain" of O.J.'s blood evidence was when there was no source for any of it!? O.J. had a thorough physical examination at the LAPD on 06/13/94. Questions such as these informed the author's investigation.

The author's approach in probing into the case was in the mode of Sir Conan Doyle's fictional character, *Sherlock Holmes*, whose axiom in *The Blanched Soldier* says: **"When you have eliminated all which is impossible, then whatever remains, however improbable, must be the truth.".**

And what remains fits! And if it fits, you must convict!!

Printed in Great Britain
by Amazon

21937832R00098